Inadequate Equilibria

Where and How Civilizations Get Stuck

ELIEZER YUDKOWSKY

Written by Eliezer Yudkowsky

Published in 2017 by the
Machine Intelligence Research Institute
Berkeley 94704
United States of America
intelligence.org

Cover artwork and design by Jimmy Rintjema

ISBN-13: 978-1-939311-22-1

Contents

Preface and Acknowledgments

Inadequate Equilibria is a book about a generalized notion of efficient markets, and how we can use this notion to guess where society will or won't be effective at pursuing some widely desired goal.

An efficient market is one where smart individuals should generally doubt that they can spot overpriced or underpriced assets. We can ask an analogous question, however, about the "efficiency" of other human endeavors.

Suppose, for example, that someone thinks they can easily build a much better and more profitable social network than Facebook, or easily come up with a new treatment for a widespread medical condition. Should they question whatever clever reasoning led them to that conclusion, in the same way that most smart individuals should question any clever reasoning that causes them to think AAPL stock is underpriced? Should they question whether they can "beat the market" in these areas, or whether they can even spot major in-principle improvements to the status quo? How "efficient," or *adequate*, should we expect civilization to be at various tasks?

There will be, as always, good ways and bad ways to reason about these questions; this book is about both. I think that generalized notions of efficiency are the primary key to good reasoning about these real-life questions. And it is often wiser to spend more time thinking about good reasoning than bad reasoning, and to lay the good foundations first. So generalized notions of efficiency and inefficiency take priority in explanation; they are the topic of the first half of this book.

The second half of this book will then delve into background questions of mindset and methodology going into inadequacy analysis, and ways that this analysis can go wrong, particularly for the underconfident.

Several of my co-workers have been invaluable to the task of editing this book: Rob Bensinger, Matthew Graves, Jimmy Rintjema, and Nate

Soares. I am also grateful to Scott Aaronson, Michael Arc, Stuart Armstrong, Bryan Caplan, Andrew Critch, Spencer Greenberg, Robin Hanson, Roxanne Heston, Ben Hoffman, Holden Karnofsky, Michael Keenan, Dan Keys, Peter McCluskey, Alex Mennen, Luke Muehlhauser, Toby Ord, Anna Salamon, Buck Shlegeris, Carl Shulman, Alyssa Vance, Qiaochu Yuan, and the many other thoughtful reviewers who provided comments and critiques. Any remaining inadequacies in this volume are my own.

—Eliezer Yudkowsky
September 2017

1. Inadequacy and Modesty

This is a book about two incompatible views on the age-old question: "When should I think that I may be able to do something *unusually well?*"

These two viewpoints tend to give wildly different, nearly *cognitively nonoverlapping* analyses of questions like:

- My doctor says I need to eat less and exercise, but a lot of educated-sounding economics bloggers are talking about this thing called the "Shangri-La Diet." They're saying that in order to lose weight, all you need to do is consume large quantities of flavorless, high-calorie foods at particular times of day; and they claim some amazing results with this diet. *Could they really know better than my doctor? Would I be able to tell if they did?*

- My day job is in artificial intelligence and decision theory. And I recall the dark days before 2015, when there was plenty of effort and attention going into advancing the state of the art in AI capabilities, but almost none going into AI alignment: better understanding AI designs and goals that can safely scale with capabilities. Though interest in the alignment problem has since increased quite a bit, it still makes sense to ask whether *at the time* I should have inferred from the lack of academic activity that there was no productive work to be done here; since *if there were reachable fruits, wouldn't academics be taking them?*

- Should I try my hand at becoming an entrepreneur? Whether or not it should be difficult to spot promising ideas in a scientific field, it certainly can't be easy to think up a profitable idea for a new startup. *Will I be able to find any good ideas that aren't already taken?*

1

- The effective altruism community is a network of philanthropists and researchers that try to find the very best ways to benefit others per dollar, in full generality. Where should effective altruism organizations like GiveWell expect to find low-hanging fruit—neglected interventions ripe with potential? *Where should they look to find things that our civilization isn't already doing about as well as can be done?*

When I think about problems like these, I use what feels to me like a natural generalization of the economic idea of efficient markets. The goal is to predict what kinds of efficiency we should expect to exist in realms beyond the marketplace, and what we can deduce from simple observations. For lack of a better term, I will call this kind of thinking *inadequacy analysis.*

Toward the end of this book, I'll try to refute an alternative viewpoint that is increasingly popular among some of my friends, one that I think is ill-founded. This viewpoint is the one I've previously termed "modesty," and the message of modesty tends to be: "You can't expect to be able to do *X* that isn't usually done, since you could just be deluding yourself into thinking you're better than other people."

I'll open with a cherry-picked example that I think helps highlight the difference between these two viewpoints.

i.

I once wrote a report, "Intelligence Explosion Microeconomics," that called for an estimate of the economic growth rate in a fully developed country— that is, a country that is no longer able to improve productivity just by importing well-tested innovations. A footnote of the paper remarked that even though Japan was the country with the most advanced technology—e.g., their cellphones and virtual reality technology were five years ahead of the rest of the world's—I wasn't going to use Japan as my estimator for developed economic growth, because, as I saw it, Japan's monetary policy was utterly deranged.

Roughly, Japan's central bank wasn't creating enough money. I won't go into details here.

A friend of mine, and one of the most careful thinkers I know—let's call him "John"—made a comment on my draft to this effect:

> How do you claim to know this? I can think of plenty of other reasons why Japan could be in a slump: the country's shrinking and aging population, its low female workplace participation, its high levels of product market regulation, etc. It looks like you're venturing outside of your area of expertise to no good end.

"How do you claim to know this?" is a very reasonable question here. As John later elaborated, macroeconomics is an area where data sets tend to be thin and predictive performance tends to be poor. And John had previously observed me making contrarian claims where I'd turned out to be badly wrong, like endorsing Gary Taubes' theories about the causes of the obesity epidemic. More recently, John won money off of me by betting that AI performance on certain metrics would improve faster than I expected; John has a good track record when it comes to spotting my mistakes.

It's also easy to imagine reasons an observer might have been skeptical. I wasn't making up my critique of Japan myself; I was reading other economists and deciding that I trusted the ones who were saying that the Bank of Japan was doing it wrong... ... Yet one would expect the governing board of the Bank of Japan to be composed of experienced economists with specialized monetary expertise. How likely is it that any outsider would be able to spot an obvious flaw in their policy? How likely is it that someone who isn't a professional economist (e.g., me) would be able to judge which economic critiques of the Bank of Japan were correct, or which critics were wise?

How likely is it that an entire country—one of the world's most advanced countries—would forego trillions of dollars of real economic growth because their monetary controllers—not politicians, but appointees from the professional elite—were doing something so wrong that even a non-professional could tell? How likely is it that a non-professional could not just suspect that the Bank of Japan was doing something badly wrong, but be *confident* in that assessment?

Surely it would be more *realistic* to search for possible reasons why the Bank of Japan might not be as stupid as it seemed, as stupid as some econbloggers were claiming. Possibly Japan's aging population made growth impossible. Possibly Japan's massive outstanding government debt made even the slightest inflation too dangerous. Possibly we just aren't thinking of the complicated reasoning going into the Bank of Japan's decision.

Surely some *humility* is appropriate when criticizing the elite decisionmakers governing the Bank of Japan. What if it's you, and not the professional economists making these decisions, who have failed to grasp the relevant economic considerations?

I'll refer to this genre of arguments as "modest epistemology."

In conversation, John clarified to me that he rejects this genre of arguments; but I hear these kinds of arguments fairly often. The head of an effective altruism organization once gave voice to what I would consider a good example of this mode of thinking:

> I find it helpful to admit to unpleasant facts that will necessarily be true in the abstract, in order to be more willing to acknowledge them in specific cases. For instance, I should expect a priori to be below average at half of things, and be 50% likely to be of below average talent overall; to know many people who I regard as better than me according to my values; to regularly make decisions that look silly ex post, and also ex ante; to be mistaken about issues on which there is expert disagreement about half of the time; to perform badly at many things I attempt for the first time; and so on.

The Dunning-Kruger effect shows that unskilled individuals often rate their own skill very highly. Specifically, although there does tend to be a correlation between how competent a person is and how competent they *guess* they are, this correlation is weaker than one might suppose. In the original study, people in the bottom two quartiles of actual test performance tended to think they did better than about 60% of test-takers, while people in the top two quartiles tended to think they did better than 70% of test-takers.

This suggests that a typical person's guesses about how they did on a test are evidence, but not particularly powerful evidence: the top quartile is underconfident in how well they did, and the bottom quartiles are highly overconfident.

Given all that, how can we gain much evidence from our belief that we are skilled? Wouldn't it be more prudent to remind ourselves of the base rate—the prior probability of 50% that we are below average?

Reasoning along similar lines, software developer Hal Finney has endorsed "abandoning personal judgment on most matters in favor of the majority view." Finney notes that the *average* person's opinions would be more accurate (on average) if they simply deferred to the most popular position on as many issues as they could. For this reason:

> I choose to adopt the view that in general, on most issues, the average opinion of humanity will be a better and less biased guide to the truth than my own judgment.
>
> […] I would suggest that although one might not always want to defer to the majority opinion, it should be the default position. Rather than starting with the assumption that one's own opinion is right, and then looking to see if the majority has good reasons for holding some other view, one should instead start off by following the majority opinion; and then only adopt a different view for good and convincing reasons. On most issues, the default of deferring to the majority will be the best approach. If we accept the principle that "extraordinary claims require extraordinary evidence", we should demand a high degree of justification for

departing from the majority view. The mere fact that our own opinion seems sound would not be enough.[1]

In this way, Finney hopes to correct for overconfidence and egocentric biases.

Finney's view is an extreme case, but helps illustrate a pattern that I believe can be found in some more moderate and widely endorsed views. When I speak of "modesty," I have in mind a fairly diverse set of positions that rest on a similar set of arguments and motivations.

I once heard an Oxford effective altruism proponent crisply summarize what I take to be the central argument for this perspective: "You see that someone says X, which seems wrong, so you conclude their epistemic standards are bad. But they could just see that you say Y, which sounds wrong to them, and conclude your epistemic standards are bad."[2] On this line of thinking, you don't get any information about who has better epistemic standards merely by observing that someone disagrees with you. After all, the other side observes just the same fact of disagreement.

Applying this argument form to the Bank of Japan example: I receive little or no evidence just from observing that the Bank of Japan says "X" when I believe "not X." I also can't be getting strong evidence from any object-level impression I might have that I am unusually competent. So did my priors imply that I and I alone ought to have been born with awesome powers of discernment? (Modest people have posed this exact question to me on more than one occasion.)

It should go without saying that this isn't how I would explain my own reasoning. But if I reject arguments of the form, "We disagree, therefore I'm right and you're wrong," how can I claim to be correct on an economic question where I disagree with an institution as reputable as the Bank of Japan?

---

[1] See Finney, "Philosophical Majoritarianism" (https://www.overcomingbias.com/2007/03/on_majoritarian.html).

[2] Note: They later said that I'd misunderstood their intent, so take this example with some grains of salt.

The other viewpoint, opposed to modesty—the view that I think is pre-scribed by normative epistemology (and also by more or less mainstream microeconomics)—requires a somewhat longer introduction.

ii.

By ancient tradition, every explanation of the Efficient Markets Hypothesis must open with the following joke:

> Two economists are walking along the street, and one says, "Hey, someone dropped a $20 bill!" and the other says, "Well, it can't be a real $20 bill because someone would have picked it up already."

Also by ancient tradition, the next step of the explanation is to remark that while it may make sense to pick up a $20 bill you see on a relatively deserted street, if you think you have spotted a $20 bill lying on the floor of Grand Central Station (the main subway nexus of New York City), and it has stayed there for several hours, then it probably *is* a fake $20 bill, or it has been glued to the ground.

In real life, when I asked a group of twenty relatively young people how many of them had ever found a $20 bill on the street, five raised their hands, and only one person had found a $20 bill on the street on two separate occasions. So the empirical truth about the joke is that while $20 bills on the street do exist, they're rare.

On the other hand, the implied policy is that if you do find a $20 bill on the street, you should go ahead and pick it up, because that does happen. It's not *that* rare. You certainly shouldn't start agonizing over whether it's too arrogant to believe that you have better eyesight than everyone else who has recently walked down the street.

On the other other hand, you *should* start agonizing about whether to trust your own mental processes if you think you've seen a $20 bill stay put for several hours on the floor of Grand Central Station. Especially if your explanation is that nobody else is eager for money.

Is there any other domain such that if we *think* we see an exploitable possibility, we should sooner doubt our own mental competence than trust the conclusion we reasoned our way to?

If I had to name the *single* epistemic feat at which modern human civilization is most adequate, the peak of all human power of estimation, I would unhesitatingly reply, "Short-term relative pricing of liquid financial assets, like the price of S&P 500 stocks relative to other S&P 500 stocks over the next three months." This is something into which human civilization puts an *actual effort*.

- Millions of dollars are offered to smart, conscientious people with physics PhDs to induce them to enter the field.

- These people are then offered huge additional payouts conditional on actual performance—especially outperformance relative to a baseline.[3]

- Large corporations form to specialize in narrow aspects of price-tuning.

- They have enormous computing clusters, vast historical datasets, and competent machine learning professionals.

- They receive repeated news of success or failure in a fast feedback loop.[4]

- The knowledge aggregation mechanism—namely, prices that equilibrate supply and demand for the financial asset—has proven to work beautifully, and acts to sum up the wisdom of all those highly motivated actors.

---

[3]This is why I specified *relative* prices: stock-trading professionals are usually graded on how well they do compared to the stock market, not compared to bonds. It's much less obvious that bonds in general are priced reasonably relative to stocks in general, though this is still being debated by economists.

[4]This is why I specified *near-term* pricing of liquid assets.

- An actor that spots a 1% systematic error in the aggregate estimate is rewarded with a billion dollars—in a process that also corrects the estimate.

- Barriers to entry are not zero (*you* can't get the loans to make a billion-dollar corrective trade), but there are thousands of diverse intelligent actors who are all individually allowed to spot errors, correct them, and be rewarded, with no central veto.

This is certainly not perfect, but it is *literally as good as it gets on modern-day Earth.*

I don't think I can beat the estimates produced by that process. I have no significant help to contribute to it. With study and effort I might become a decent hedge fundie and make a standard return. Theoretically, a liquid market should be just exploitable enough to pay competent professionals the same hourly rate as their next-best opportunity. I could potentially become one of those professionals, and earn standard hedge-fundie returns, but that's not the same as significantly improving on the market's efficiency. I'm not sure I expect a huge humanly accessible opportunity of that kind to *exist,* not in the thickly traded centers of the market. Somebody *really would* have taken it already! Our civilization *cares* about whether Microsoft stock will be priced at $37.70 or $37.75 tomorrow afternoon.

I can't predict a 5% move in Microsoft stock in the next two months, and *neither can you.* If your uncle tells an anecdote about how he tripled his investment in NetBet.com last year and he attributes this to his skill rather than luck, we know *immediately and out of hand* that he is wrong. Warren Buffett at the peak of his form couldn't reliably triple his money every year. If there is a strategy so simple that your uncle can understand it, which has apparently made him money—then we guess that there were just hidden risks built into the strategy, and that in another year or with less favorable events he would have lost half as much as he gained. Any other possibility would be the equivalent of a $20 bill staying on the floor of Grand Central

Station for ten years while a horde of physics PhDs searched for it using naked eyes, microscopes, and machine learning.

In the thickly traded parts of the stock market, where the collective power of human civilization is truly at its strongest, I doff my hat, I put aside my pride and kneel in true humility to accept the market's beliefs as though they were my own, knowing that any impulse I feel to second-guess and every independent thought I have to argue otherwise is nothing but my own folly. If my perceptions suggest an exploitable opportunity, then my perceptions are far more likely mistaken than the markets. That is what it feels like to look upon a civilization doing something adequately.

The converse side of the efficient-markets perspective would have said this about the Bank of Japan:

CONVENTIONAL CYNICAL ECONOMIST: So, Eliezer, you think you know better than the Bank of Japan and many other central banks around the world, do you?

ELIEZER: Yep. Or rather, by reading econblogs, I believe myself to have identified which econbloggers know better, like Scott Sumner.

C.C.E.: Even though literally trillions of dollars of real value are at stake?

ELIEZER: Yep.

C.C.E.: How do you make money off this special knowledge of yours?

ELIEZER: I can't. The market also collectively knows that the Bank of Japan is pursuing a bad monetary policy and has priced Japanese equities accordingly. So even though I know the Bank of Japan's policy will make Japanese equities perform badly, that fact is already priced in; I can't expect to make money by short-selling Japanese equities.

C.C.E.: I see. So exactly who is it, on this theory of yours, that is being stupid and passing up a predictable payout?

ELIEZER: Nobody, of course! Only the Bank of Japan is allowed to control the trend line of the Japanese money supply, and the Bank of Japan's governors are not paid any bonuses when the Japanese economy does better. They don't get a million dollars in personal bonuses if the Japanese economy grows by a trillion dollars.

C.C.E.: So you can't make any money off knowing better individually, and nobody who has the actual power and authority to fix the problem would gain a personal financial benefit from fixing it? Then we're done! No anomalies here; this sounds like a perfectly normal state of affairs.

We don't usually expect to find $20 bills lying on the street, because even though people sometimes drop $20 bills, someone else will usually have a chance to pick up that $20 bill before we do.

We don't think we can predict 5% price changes in S&P 500 company stock prices over the next month, because we're competing against dozens of hedge fund managers with enormous supercomputers and physics PhDs, any one of whom could make millions or billions on the pricing error—and in doing so, correct that error.

We can expect it to be hard to come up with a truly good startup idea, and for even the best ideas to involve sweat and risk, because lots of other people are trying to think up good startup ideas. Though in this case we do have the advantage that we can pick our own battles, seek out *one* good idea that we think hasn't been done yet.

But the Bank of Japan is just one committee, and it's not possible for anyone else to step up and make a billion dollars in the course of correcting their error. Even if you think you know exactly what the Bank of Japan is doing wrong, you can't make a profit on that. At least some hedge-fund managers also know what the Bank of Japan is doing wrong, and the expected consequences are already priced into the market. Nor does this price movement fix the Bank of Japan's mistaken behavior. So to the extent the Bank of Japan has poor incentives or some other systematic dysfunction, their mistake can persist. As a consequence, when I read some econbloggers who I'd seen being right about empirical predictions before saying that Japan was being grotesquely silly, and the economic logic seemed to me to check out, as best I could follow it, I wasn't particularly reluctant to believe them. *Standard economic theory, generalized beyond the markets to other facets of society, did not seem to me to predict that the Bank of Japan must act wisely for the good of Japan.* It would be no surprise if they were competent, but also not much of a surprise if they were incompetent. And knowing this didn't help me either—I couldn't exploit the knowledge to make an excess profit myself—and this too wasn't a coincidence.

This kind of thinking can get quite a bit more complicated than the foregoing paragraphs might suggest. We have to ask why the government of Japan didn't put pressure on the Bank of Japan (answer: they did, but the Bank of Japan refused), and many other questions. You would need to consider a much larger model of the world, and bring in a lot more background theory, to be confident that you understood the overall situation with the Bank of Japan.

But even without that detailed analysis, in the epistemological background we have a completely different picture from the modest one. We have a picture of the world where it is perfectly plausible for an econblogger to write up a good analysis of what the Bank of Japan is doing wrong, and for a sophisticated reader to reasonably agree that the analysis seems decisive, without a deep agonizing episode of Dunning-Kruger-inspired self-doubt playing any important role in the analysis.

iii.

When we critique a government, we don't usually get to see what would actually happen if the government took our advice. But in this one case, less than a month after my exchange with John, the Bank of Japan—under the new leadership of Haruhiko Kuroda, and under unprecedented pressure from recently elected Prime Minister Shinzo Abe, who included monetary policy in his campaign platform—embarked on an attempt to print huge amounts of money, with a stated goal of doubling the Japanese money supply.[5]

Immediately after, Japan experienced real GDP growth of 2.3%, where the previous trend was for falling RGDP. Their economy was operating that far under capacity due to lack of money.[6]

Now, on the modest view, this was the unfairest test imaginable. Out of all the times that I've ever suggested that a government's policy is suboptimal, the rare time a government tries my preferred alternative will select the most mainstream, highest-conventional-prestige policies I happen to advocate, and those are the very policy proposals that modesty is least likely to disapprove of.

Indeed, if John had looked further into the issue, he would have found (as I found while writing this) that Nobel laureates had also criticized Japan's monetary policy. He would have found that previous Japanese governments had also hinted to the Bank of Japan that they should print more money. The view from modesty looks at this state of affairs and says, "Hold up! You aren't so specially blessed as your priors would have you believe; other academics already know what you know! Civilization isn't so inadequate after all! This

---

[5]That is, the Bank of Japan purchased huge numbers of bonds with newly created electronic money.

[6]See "How Japan Proved Printing Money Can Be A Great Idea" (https://www.washingtonpost.com/news/wonk/wp/2017/05/16/how-japan-proved-printing-money-can-be-a-great-idea/) for a more recent update.

For readers who are wondering, "Wait, how the heck can printing money possibly lead to real goods and services being created?" I suggest Googling "sticky wages" and possibly consulting Scott Sumner's history of the Great Depression, *The Midas Paradox.*

is how reasonable dissent from established institutions and experts operates in the real world: via opposition by other mainstream experts and institutions, not via the heroic effort of a lone economics blogger."

However helpful or unhelpful such remarks may be for guarding against inflated pride, however, they don't seem to refute (or even address) the central thesis of civilizational *inadequacy*, as I will define that term later. Roughly, the civilizational inadequacy thesis states that in situations where the central bank of a major developed democracy is carrying out a policy, and a number of highly regarded economists like Ben Bernanke have written papers about what that central bank is doing wrong, and there are widely accepted macroeconomic theories for understanding what that central bank is doing wrong, and the government of the country has tried to put pressure on the central bank to stop doing it wrong, and literally *trillions* of dollars in real wealth are at stake, then *the overall competence of human civilization* is such that we shouldn't be surprised to find the professional economists at the Bank of Japan doing it wrong.

We shouldn't even be surprised to find that a decision theorist without all that much background in economics can identify which econbloggers have correctly stated what the Bank of Japan is doing wrong, or which simple improvements to their current policies would improve the situation.

iv.

It doesn't make much difference to my life whether I understand monetary policy better than, say, the European Central Bank, which as of late 2015 was repeating the same textbook mistake as the Bank of Japan and causing trillions of euros of damage to the European economy. Insofar as I have other European friends in countries like Italy, it might be important to them to know that Europe's economy is probably not going to get any better soon; or the knowledge might be relevant to predicting AI progress timelines to know whether Japan ran out of low-hanging technological fruit or just had bad monetary policy. But that's a rather distant relevance, and for most of my readers I would expect this issue to be even less relevant to their lives.

But you run into the same implicit background questions of inadequacy analysis when, for example, you're making health care decisions. Cherry-picking another anecdote: My wife has a severe case of Seasonal Affective Disorder. As of 2014, she'd tried sitting in front of a little lightbox for an hour per day, and it hadn't worked. SAD's effects were crippling enough for it to be worth our time to consider extreme options, like her spending time in South America during the winter months. And indeed, vacationing in Chile and receiving more exposure to actual sunlight *did* work, where lightboxes failed.

From my perspective, the obvious next thought was: "Empirically, dinky little lightboxes don't work. Empirically, the Sun does work. Next step: *more light.* Fill our house with more lumens than lightboxes provide." In short order, I had strung up sixty-five 60W-equivalent LED bulbs in the living room, and another sixty-five in her bedroom.

Ah, but should I assume that my civilization is being *opportunistic* about seeking out ways to cure SAD, and that if putting up 130 LED light bulbs often worked when lightboxes failed, *doctors would already know about that?* Should the fact that putting up 130 light bulbs isn't a well-known next step after lightboxes convince me that my bright idea is probably not a good idea, because if it were, everyone would already be doing it? Should I conclude from my inability to find any published studies on the Internet testing this question that there is some fatal flaw in my plan that I'm just not seeing?

We might call this argument "Chesterton's Absence of a Fence." The thought being: I shouldn't build a fence here, because if it were a good idea to have a fence here, someone would already have built it. The underlying question here is: How strongly should I expect that this extremely common medical problem has been thoroughly considered by my civilization, and that there's nothing new, effective, and unconventional that I can personally improvise?

Eyeballing this question, my off-the-cuff answer—based mostly on the impressions related to me by every friend of mine who has ever dealt with medicine on a research level—is that I wouldn't *necessarily* expect any medical researcher ever to have done a formal experiment on the first thought that popped into my mind for treating this extremely common depressive syndrome. Nor would I strongly expect the intervention, if initial tests found it to be effective, to have received enough attention that I could Google it.

But this is just my personal take on the adequacy of 21st-century medical research. Should I be nervous that this line of thinking is just an excuse? Should I fret about the apparently high estimate of my own competence implied by my thinking that I could find an obvious-seeming way to remedy SAD when *trained doctors* aren't talking about it and I'm not a medical researcher? Am I going too far outside my own area of expertise and starting to think that I'm good at everything?

In practice, I didn't bother going through an agonizing fit of self-doubt along those lines. The systematic competence of human civilization with respect to treating mood disorders wasn't so apparent to me that I considered it a better use of resources to quietly drop the issue than to just lay down the ~$600 needed to test my suspicion. So I went ahead and ran the experiment. And as of early 2017, with two winters come and gone, Brienne seems to no longer have crippling SAD—though it took a *lot* of light bulbs, including light bulbs in her bedroom that had to be timed to go on at 7:30am before she woke up, to sustain the apparent cure.[7]

If you want to outperform—if you want to do anything not usually done— then you'll need to conceptually divide our civilization into areas of lower and greater competency. My view is that this is best done from a framework

---

[7]Specifically, Brienne's symptoms were mostly cured in the winter of 2015, and partially cured in the winter of 2016, when she spent most of her time under fewer lights. Brienne reports that she suffered a lot less even in the more recent winter, and experienced no suicidal ideation, unlike in years prior to the light therapy.

I'll be moderately surprised if this treatment works *reliably*, just because most things don't where depression is concerned; but I would predict that it works often enough to be worth trying for other people experiencing severe treatment-resistant SAD.

of incentives and the equilibria of those incentives—which is to say, from the standpoint of microeconomics. This is the main topic I'll cover here.

In the process, I will also make the case that modesty—the part of this process where you go into an agonizing fit of self-doubt—isn't actually helpful for figuring out when you might outperform some aspect of the equilibrium.

But one should initially present a positive agenda in discussions like these— saying first what you think is the correct epistemology, before inveighing against a position you think is wrong.

So without further ado, in the next chapter I shall present a very simple framework for inadequate equilibria.

2. An Equilibrium of No Free Energy

I am now going to introduce some concepts that lack established names in the economics literature—though I don't believe that any of the basic ideas are new to economics.

First, I want to distinguish between the standard economic concept of *efficiency* (as in efficient pricing) and the related but distinct concepts of *inexploitability* and *adequacy*, which are what usually matter in real life.

i.

Depending on the strength of your filter bubble, you may have met people who become angry when they hear the phrase "efficient markets," taking the expression to mean that hedge fund managers are particularly wise, or that markets are particularly just.[8]

Part of where this interpretation appears to be coming from is a misconception that market prices reflect a judgment on anyone's part about what price would be "best"—fairest, say, or kindest.

In a pre-market economy, when you offer somebody fifty carrots for a roasted antelope leg, your offer says something about how impressed you are with their work hunting down the antelope and how much reward you think that deserves from you. If they've dealt generously with you in the past, perhaps you ought to offer them more. This is the only instinctive notion people start with for what a price could mean: a personal interaction between Alice and Bob reflecting past friendships and a balance of social judgments.

---

[8]If the person gets angry and starts talking about lack of liquidity, rather than about the pitfalls of capitalism, then that is an entirely separate class of dispute.

In contrast, the economic notion of a market price is that for every loaf of bread bought, there is a loaf of bread sold; and therefore actual demand and actual supply are always equal. The market price is the input that makes the decreasing curve for demand as a function of price meet the increasing curve for supply as a function of price. This price is an "is" statement rather than an "ought" statement, an observation and not a wish.

In particular, an efficient market, from an economist's perspective, is just one whose average price movement can't be predicted by you.

If that way of putting it sounds odd, consider an analogy. Suppose you asked a well-designed superintelligent AI system to estimate how many hydrogen atoms are in the Sun. You don't expect the superintelligence to produce an answer that is *exactly right* down to the last atom, because this would require measuring the mass of the Sun more finely than any measuring instrument you expect it to possess. At the same time, it would be very odd for you to say, "Well, I think the superintelligence will underestimate the number of atoms in the Sun by 10%, because hydrogen atoms are very light and the AI system might not take that into account." Yes, hydrogen atoms are light, but the AI system knows that too. Any reason you can devise for how a superintelligence could underestimate the amount of hydrogen in the Sun is a possibility that the superintelligence can also see and take into account. So while you don't expect the system to get the answer exactly right, you don't expect that you *yourself* will be able to predict the *average value* of the error—to predict that the system will underestimate the amount by 10%, for example.

This is the property that an economist thinks an "efficient" price has. An efficient price can update sharply: the company can do worse or better than expected, and the stock can move sharply up or down on the news. In some cases, you can rationally expect volatility; you can predict that good news might arrive tomorrow and make the stock go up, balanced by a counter-possibility that the news will fail to arrive and the stock will go down. You could think the stock is 30% likely to rise by $10 and 20% likely to drop by $15 and 50% likely to stay the same. But you can't predict in advance the *average value* by which the price will change, which is what it would take to make an expected profit by buying the stock or short-selling it.[9]

When an economist says that a market price is efficient over a two-year time horizon, they mean: "The current price that balances the supply and demand of this financial instrument well reflects all public information affecting a boundedly rational estimate of the future supply-demand balancing point of this financial instrument in two years." They're relating the present intersection of these two curves to an idealized cognitive estimate of the curves' future intersection.

But this is a long sentence in the language of a hunter-gatherer. If somebody doesn't have all the terms of that sentence precompiled in their head, then they're likely to interpret the sentence in the idiom of ordinary human life and ordinary human relationships.

People have an innate understanding of "true" in the sense of a map that reflects the territory, and they can imagine processes that produce good maps; but probability and microeconomics are less intuitive.[10] What people hear when you talk about "efficient prices" is that a cold-blooded machine has determined that some people ought to be paid \$9/hour. And they hear the economist saying nice things about the machine, praising it as "efficient," implying that the machine is *right* about this \$9/hour price being good for society, that this price well reflects what someone's efforts are justly worth. They hear you agreeing with this pitiless machine's judgment about how the

---

[9]You can often predict the likely *direction* of a move in such a market, even though on average your best guess for the change in price will always be 0. This is because the median market move will usually not equal the mean market move.

For similar reasons, a rational agent *can* usually predict the direction of a future Bayesian update, even though the average value by which their probability changes should be 0. A high probability of a small update in the expected direction can be offset by a low probability of a larger update in the opposite direction.

[10]Anyone who tries to spread probability literacy quickly runs into the problem that a weather forecast giving an 80% chance of clear skies is deemed "wrong" on the 1-in-5 occasions when it in fact rains, prompting people to wonder what mistake the weather forecaster made this time around.

intuitive web of obligations and incentives and reputation ought properly to cash out for a human interaction.

And in the domain of stocks, when stock prices are observed to swing widely, this intuitive view says that the market can't be that smart after all. For if it were smart, would it keep turning out to be "wrong" and need to change its mind?

I once read a rather clueless magazine article that made fun of a political prediction market on the basis that when a new poll came out, the price of the prediction market moved. "It just tracks the polls!" the author proclaimed. But the point of the prediction market is not that it knows some fixed, objective chance with high accuracy. The point of a prediction market is that it summarizes all the information available to the market participants. If the poll moved prices, then the poll was new information that the market thought was important, and the market updated its belief, and this is just the way things should be.

In a liquid market, "price moves whose average direction you can predict in advance" correspond to both "places you can make a profit" and "places where you know better than the market." A market that knows everything you know is a market where prices are "efficient" in the conventional economic sense—one where you can't predict the net direction in which the price will change.

This means that the efficiency of a market is assessed relative to your own intelligence, which is fine. Indeed, it's possible that the concept should be called "relative efficiency." Yes, a superintelligence might be able to predict price trends that no modern human hedge fund manager could; but economists don't think that today's markets are efficient relative to a superintelligence.

Today's markets may not be efficient relative to the smartest hedge fund managers, or efficient relative to corporate insiders with secret knowledge that hasn't yet leaked. But the stock markets are efficient relative to you, and to me, and to your Uncle Albert who thinks he tripled his money through his incredible acumen in buying NetBet.com.

Not everything that involves a financial price is efficient. There was recently a startup called Color Labs, aka Color.com, whose putative purpose was to let people share photos with their friends and see other photos that had been taken nearby. They closed $41 million in funding, including $20 million from the prestigious Sequoia Capital.

When the news of their funding broke, practically everyone on the online Hacker News forum was rolling their eyes and predicting failure. It seemed like a nitwit me-too idea to me too. And then, yes, Color Labs failed and the 20-person team sold themselves to Apple for $7 million and the venture capitalists didn't make back their money. And yes, it sounds to me like the prestigious Sequoia Capital bought into the wrong startup.

If that's all true, it's not a coincidence that neither I nor any of the other onlookers could make money on our advance prediction. The startup equity market was *inefficient* (a price underwent a predictable decline), but it wasn't *exploitable*.[11] There was no way to make a profit just by predicting that Sequoia had overpaid for the stock it bought. Because, at least as of 2017, the market lacks a certain type and direction of liquidity: you can't short-sell startup equity.[12]

What about houses? Millions of residential houses change hands every year, and they cost more than stock shares. If we expect the stock market to be well-priced, shouldn't we expect the same of houses?

The answer is "no," because you can't short-sell a house. Sure, there are some ways to bet against aggregate housing markets, like shorting real estate investment trusts or home manufacturers. But in the end, hedge

---

[11] More precisely, I would say that the market was inexploitable in money, but inefficiently priced.

[12] To short-sell is to borrow the asset, sell it, and then buy it back later after the price declines; or sometimes to create a synthetic copy of an asset, so you can sell that. Shorting an asset allows you to make money if the price goes down in the future, and has the effect of lowering the asset's price by increasing supply.

fund managers can't make a synthetic financial instrument that behaves just like the house on 6702 West St. and sell it into the same housing market frequented by consumers like you. Which is why you might do very well to think for yourself about whether the price seems sensible to you before buying a house: because you might know better than the market price, even as a non-specialist relying only on publicly available information.

Let's imagine there are 100,000 houses in Boomville, of which 10,000 have been for sale in the last year or so. Suppose there are 20,000 fools who think that housing prices in Boomville can only go up, and 10,000 rational hedge fund managers who think that the shale-oil business may collapse and lead to a predictable decline in Boomville house prices. There's no way for the hedge fund managers to short Boomville house prices—not in a way that satisfies the optimistic demand of 20,000 fools for Boomville houses, not in a way that causes house prices to actually decline. The 20,000 fools just bid on the 10,000 available houses until the skyrocketing price of the houses makes 10,000 of the fools give up.

Some smarter agents might decline to buy, and so somewhat reduce demand. But the smarter agents can't actually visit Boomville and make hundreds of thousands of dollars off of the overpriced houses. The price *is* too high and *will* predictably decline, relative to public information, but there's no way you can make a profit on knowing that. An individual who owns an existing house can exploit the inefficiency by selling that house, but rational market actors can't crowd around the inefficiency and exploit it until it's all gone.

Whereas a predictably *underpriced* house, put on the market for predictably much less than its future price, would be an asset that any of a hundred thousand rational investors could come in and snap up.

So a frothy housing market may see many overpriced houses, but few underpriced ones.

Thus it will be easy to lose money in this market by buying stupidly, and much harder to make money by buying cleverly. The market prices will be *inefficient*—in a certain sense stupid—but they will not be *exploitable*.

In contrast, in a thickly traded market where it is easy to short an over-priced asset, prices will be efficient in both directions, and any day is as good a day to buy as any other. You may end up exposed to excess *volatility* (an asset with a 50% chance of doubling and a 50% chance of going bankrupt, for example), but you won't actually have bought anything overpriced—if it were predictably overpriced, it would have been short-sold.[13]

We can see the notion of an inexploitable market as generalizing the notion of an efficient market as follows: in both cases, *there's no free energy inside the system*. In both markets, there's a horde of hungry organisms moving around trying to eat up all the free energy. In the efficient market, *every predictable price change corresponds to free energy* (easy money) and so the equilibrium where hungry organisms have eaten all the free energy corresponds to an equilibrium of no predictable price changes. In a merely inexploitable market, there are predictable price changes that don't correspond to free energy, like an overpriced house that will decline later, and so the no-free-energy equilibrium can still involve predictable price changes.[14]

---

[13] Though beware that even in a stock market, some stocks are harder to short than others—like stocks that have just IPOed. Drechsler and Drechsler found that creating a broad market fund of only *assets that are easy to short* in recent years would have produced 5% higher returns (!) than index funds that don't kick out hard-to-short assets (https://papers.ssrn.com/sol3/papers.cfm?abstract_id=2387099). Unfortunately, I don't know of any index fund that actually tracks this strategy, or it's what I'd own as my main financial asset.

[14] Robert Shiller (https://www.nytimes.com/2015/07/26/upshot/the-housing-market-still-isnt-rational.html) cites Edward Miller (https://onlinelibrary.wiley.com/doi/10.1111/j.1540-6261.1977.tb03317.x/abstract) as having observed in 1977 that efficiency requires short sales, and either Shiller or Miller observes that houses can't be shorted. But I don't know of any standard economic term for markets that are inefficient but "inexploitable" (as I termed it). It's not a new idea, but I don't know if it has an old name.

I mention parenthetically that a regulator that genuinely and deeply cared about protecting retail financial customers would just concentrate on making everything in that market easy to short-sell. This is the obvious and only way to ensure the asset is not overpriced. If the Very Serious People behind the JOBS Act to enable crowdfunded startups had honestly wanted to protect normal people and understood this phenomenon, they would mandate that all equity sales go through an exchange where it was easy to bet against the equity of dumb startups, and then declare their work done and go on per-

Our ability to say, within the context of the general theory of "efficient markets," that houses in Boomville may still be overpriced—and, additionally, to say that they are much less likely to be underpriced—is what makes this style of reasoning powerful. It doesn't just say, "Prices are usually right when lots of money is flowing." It gives us detailed conditions for when we should and shouldn't expect efficiency. There's an underlying logic about powerfully smart organisms, any single one of which can consume free energy if it is available in worthwhile quantities, in a way that produces a global equilibrium of no free energy; and if one of the premises is invalidated, we get a different prediction.

iii.

At one point during the 2016 presidential election, the PredictIt prediction market—the only one legally open to US citizens (and only US citizens)—had Hillary Clinton at a 60% probability of winning the general election. The bigger, international prediction market BetFair had Clinton at 80% at that time.

So I looked into buying Clinton shares on PredictIt—but discovered, alas, that PredictIt charged a 10% fee on profits, a 5% fee on withdrawals, had an $850 limit per contract bet... and on top of all that, I'd also have to pay 28% federal and 9.3% state income taxes on any gains. Which, in sum, meant I wouldn't be getting much more than $30 in expected return for the time and hassle of buying the contracts.

Oh, if only PredictIt didn't charge that 10% fee on profits, that 5% fee on withdrawals! If only they didn't have the $850 limit! If only the US didn't have such high income taxes, and didn't limit participation in overseas prediction markets! I could have bought Clinton shares at 60 cents on

---

manent vacation in Aruba. This is the easy and only way to protect consumers from overpriced financial assets.

PredictIt and Trump shares at 20 cents on Betfair, winning a dollar either way and getting a near-guaranteed 25% return until the prices were in line! Curse those silly rules, preventing me from picking up that free money!

Does that complaint sound reasonable to you?

If so, then you haven't yet fully internalized the notion of an inefficient-but-inexploitable market.

If the taxes, fees, and betting limits hadn't been there, the PredictIt and BetFair prices would have been the same.

iv.

Suppose it were the case that some cases of Seasonal Affective Disorder proved resistant to sitting in front of a 10,000-lux lightbox for 30 minutes (the standard treatment), but would nonetheless respond if you bought 130 or so 60-watt-equivalent high-CRI LED bulbs, in a mix of 5000K and 2700K color temperatures, and strung them up over your two-bedroom apartment.

Would you expect that, supposing this were true, there would already exist a journal report somewhere on it?

Would you expect that, supposing this were true, it would already be widely discussed (or at least rumored) on the Internet?

Would you expect that, supposing this were true, doctors would already know about it and it would be on standard medical pages about Seasonal Affective Disorder?

And would you, failing to observe anything on the subject after a couple of hours of Googling, conclude that your civilization must have some unknown good reason why not everyone was doing this already?

To answer a question like this, we need an analysis not of the world's efficiency or inexploitability but rather of its *adequacy*—whether all the low-hanging fruit have been plucked.

A duly modest skepticism, translated into the terms we've been using so far, might say something like this: "Around 7% of the population has severe Seasonal Affective Disorder, and another 20% or so has weak Seasonal Affective Disorder. Around 50% of tested cases respond to standard light-boxes. So if the intervention of stringing up a hundred LED bulbs actually worked, it could provide a major improvement to the lives of 3% of the US population, costing on the order of $1000 each (without economies of scale). Many of those 9 million US citizens would be rich enough to afford that as a treatment for major winter depression. If you could prove that your system worked, you could create a company to sell SAD-grade lighting systems and have a large market. So by postulating that you can cure SAD this way, you're postulating a world in which there's a huge quantity of metaphorical free energy—a big energy gradient that society hasn't traversed. Therefore, I'm skeptical of this medical theory for more or less the same reason that I'm skeptical you can make money on the stock market: it postulates a $20 bill lying around that nobody has already picked up."

So the distinction is:

- **Efficiency**: "Microsoft's stock price is neither too low nor too high, relative to anything *you* can possibly know about Microsoft's stock price."

- **Inexploitability**: "Some houses and housing markets are overpriced, but you can't make a profit by short-selling them, and you're unlikely to find any substantially *underpriced* houses—the market as a whole isn't rational, but it contains participants who have money and understand housing markets as well as you do."

- **Adequacy**: "Okay, the medical sector is a wildly crazy place where different interventions have orders-of-magnitude differences in cost-effectiveness, but at least there's no well-known but unused way to save *ten thousand lives for just ten dollars each*, right? *Somebody* would have picked up on it! Right?!"

Let's say that within some slice through society, the obvious low-hanging fruit that save *more* than ten thousand lives for less than a hundred thousand dollars total have, in fact, been picked up. Then I propose the following terminology: let us say that that part of society is *adequate* at saving 10,000 lives for $100,000.

And if there's a convincing case that this property does not hold, we'll say this subsector is *inadequate* (at saving 10,000 lives for $100,000).

To see how an inadequate equilibrium might arise, let's start by focusing on one tiny subfactor of the human system, namely academic research.

We'll even further oversimplify our model of academia and pretend that research is a two-factor system containing *academics* and *grantmakers*, and that a project can only happen if there's both a participating academic and a participating grantmaker.

We next suppose that in some academic field, there exists a population of researchers who are individually eager and collectively opportunistic for publications—papers accepted to journals, especially high-impact journal publications that constitute strong progress toward tenure. For any clearly visible opportunity to get a sufficiently large number of citations with a small enough amount of work, there are collectively enough academics in this field that somebody will snap up the opportunity. We could say, to make the example more precise, that the field is collectively opportunistic in 2 citations per workday—if there's any clearly visible opportunity to do 40 days of work and get 80 citations, somebody in the field will go for it.

This level of opportunism might be much more than the average paper gets in citations per day of work. Maybe the average is more like 10 citations per year of work, and lots of researchers work for a year on a paper that ends up garnering only 3 citations. We're not trying to ask about the *average* price of a citation; we're trying to ask how cheap a citation has to be before *somebody somewhere* is virtually *guaranteed* to try for it.

But academic paper-writers are only half the equation; the other half is a population of grantmakers.

In this model, can we suppose for argument's sake that grantmakers are motivated by the pure love of all sentient life, and yet we still end up with an academic system that is *inadequate?*

I might naively reply: "Sure. Let's say that those selfish academics are collectively opportunistic at two citations per workday, and the blameless and benevolent grantmakers are collectively opportunistic at one quality-adjusted life-year (QALY) per $100.[15] Then everything which produces one QALY per $100 *and* two citations per workday gets funded. Which means there could be an obvious, clearly visible project that would produce a thousand QALYs per dollar, and so long as it doesn't produce enough citations, nobody will work on it. That's what the model says, right?"

Ah, but this model has a *fragile* equilibrium of inadequacy. It only takes one researcher who is opportunistic in QALYs and willing to take a hit in citations to snatch up the biggest, lowest-hanging altruistic fruit if there's a population of grantmakers eager to fund projects like that.

Assume the most altruistically neglected project produces 1,000 QALYs per dollar. If we add a single rational and altruistic researcher to this model, then they will work on that project, whereupon the equilibrium will be adequate at 1,000 QALYs per dollar. If there are two rational and altruistic researchers, the second one to arrive will start work on the next-most-neglected project—say, a project that has 500 QALYs/$ but wouldn't garner enough citations for whatever reason—and then the field will be adequate at 500 QALYs/$. As this free energy gets eaten up (it's tasty energy from the perspective of an altruist eager for QALYs), the whole field becomes less inadequate in the relevant respect.

But this assumes the grantmakers are eager to fund highly efficient QALY-increasing projects.

Suppose instead that the grantmakers are *not* cause-neutral scope-sensitive effective altruists assessing QALYs/$. Suppose that most grantmakers pursue, say, *prestige per dollar*. (Robin Hanson offers an elementary argument that

---

[15] "Quality-adjusted life year" is a measure used to compare the effectiveness of medical interventions. QALYs are a popular way of relating the costs of death and disease, though they're generally defined in ways that exclude non-health contributors to quality of life.

most grantmaking to academia is about prestige.[16] In any case, we can provisionally assume the prestige model for purposes of this toy example.)

From the perspective of most grantmakers, the ideal grant is one that gets their individual name, or their boss's name, or their organization's name, in newspapers around the world in close vicinity to phrases like "Stephen Hawking" or "Harvard professor." Let's say for the purpose of this thought experiment that the population of grantmakers is collectively opportunistic in 20 microHawkings per dollar, such that at least one of them will definitely jump on any clearly visible opportunity to affiliate themselves with Stephen Hawking for $50,000. Then at equilibrium, everything that provides at least 2 citations per workday *and* 20 microHawkings per dollar will get done.

This doesn't quite follow logically, because the stock market is far more efficient at matching bids between buyers and sellers than academia is at matching researchers to grantmakers. (It's not like anyone in our civilization has put as much effort into rationalizing the academic matching process as, say, OkCupid has put into their software for hooking up dates. It's not like anyone who did produce this public good would get paid more than they could have made as a Google programmer.)

But even if the argument is still missing some pieces, you can see the general shape of this style of analysis. If a piece of research will clearly visibly yield lots of citations with a reasonable amount of labor, and make the grantmakers on the committee look good for not too much money committed, then a researcher eager to do it can probably find a grantmaker eager to fund it.

But what if there's some intervention which could save 100 QALYs/$, yet produces neither great citations nor great prestige? Then if we add a few altruistic researchers to the model, they probably won't be able to find a grantmaker to fund it; and if we add a few altruistic grantmakers to the model, they probably won't be able to find a qualified researcher to work on it.

---

[16]Hanson,   "Academia's   Function"   (https://www.overcoming-bias.com/2009/07/academias-function.html).

One systemic problem can often be overcome by one altruist in the right place. *Two* systemic problems are another matter entirely.

Usually when we find trillion-dollar bills lying on the ground in real life, it's a symptom of (1) a central-command bottleneck that nobody else is allowed to fix, as with the European Central Bank wrecking Europe, or (2) a system with enough moving parts that *at least two parts are simultaneously broken*, meaning that *single actors cannot defy the system*. To modify an old aphorism: usually, when things suck, it's because they suck in a way that's a Nash equilibrium.

In the same way that *inefficient* markets tend systematically to be *inexploitable*, grossly *inadequate* systems tend systematically to be *unfixable* by individual non-billionaires.

But then you can sometimes still insert a wedge for yourself, even if you can't save the whole system. Something that's systemically hard to fix for the whole planet is sometimes possible to fix in your own two-bedroom apartment. So inadequacy is even more important than exploitability on a day-to-day basis, because it's inadequacy-generating situations that lead to low-hanging fruits large enough to be worthwhile at the individual level.

v.

A critical analogy between an inadequate system and an efficient market is this: even systems that are horribly inadequate from our own perspective *are still in a competitive equilibrium*. There's still an equilibrium of incentives, an equilibrium of supply and demand, an equilibrium where (in the central example above) all the researchers are vigorously competing for prestigious publications and using up all available grant money in the course of doing so. There's no free energy anywhere in the system.

I've seen a number of novice rationalists committing what I shall term the Free Energy Fallacy, which is something along the lines of, "This system's purpose is supposed to be to cook omelettes, and yet it produces terrible omelettes. So why don't I use my amazing skills to cook some better omelettes and take over?"

And generally the answer is that maybe the system from *your* perspective is broken, but everyone within the system is intensely competing along *other* dimensions and you can't keep up with that competition. They're all chasing whatever things people in that system actually pursue—instead of the lost purposes they wistfully remember, but don't have a chance to pursue because it would be career suicide. You won't become competitive along those dimensions just by cooking better omelettes.

No researcher has any spare attention to give your improved omelette-cooking idea because they are already using all of their labor to try to get publications into high-impact journals; they have no free work hours.

The journals won't take your omelette-cooking paper because they get *lots* of attempted submissions that they screen, for example, by looking for whether the researcher is from a high-prestige institution or whether the paper is written in a style that makes it look technically difficult. Being good at cooking omelettes doesn't make you the *best* competitor at writing papers to appeal to prestigious journals—any publication slot would have to be given to you rather than someone else who is intensely trying to get it. Your good omelette technique might be a *bonus*, but only if you were already doing everything else right (which you're not).

The grantmakers have no free money to give you to run your omelette-cooking experiment, because there are thousands of researchers competing for their money, and you are not competitive at convincing grantmaking committees that you're a safe, reputable, prestigious option. Maybe they feel wistfully fond of the ideal of better omelettes, but it would be career suicide for them to give money to the wrong person because of that.

What inadequate systems and efficient markets have in common is the lack of any free energy in the equilibrium. We can see the equilibrium in both cases as *defined* by an absence of free energy. In an efficient market, any predictable price change corresponds to free energy, so thousands of hungry organisms trying to eat the free energy produce a lack of predictable price changes. In a system like academia, the competition for free energy may not correspond to anything good from your own standpoint, and as a result you may label the outcome "inadequate"; but there is still no free energy. Trying to feed *within* the system, or do anything within the system that uses a resource the other competing organisms want—money, publication space, prestige, attention—will generally be as hard for you as it is for any other organism.

Indeed, if the system gave priority to rewarding better performance along the most useful or socially beneficial dimensions over all competing ways of feeding, the system wouldn't be inadequate in the first place. It's like wishing PredictIt didn't have fees and betting limits so that you could snap up those mispriced contracts.

In a way, it's this very lack of free energy, this intense competition without space to draw a breath, that keeps the inadequacy around and makes it non-fragile. In the case of US science, there was a brief period after World War II where there was new funding coming in faster than universities could create new grad students, and scientists had a chance to pursue ideas that they liked. Today Malthus has reasserted himself, and it's no longer generally feasible for people to achieve career success while going off and just pursuing the research they most enjoy, or just going off and pursuing the research with the largest altruistic benefits. For any actor to do the best thing from an altruistic standpoint, they'd need to ignore all of the system's internal incentives pointing somewhere else, and there's no free energy in the system to feed someone who does that.[17]

---

[17] This is also why, for example, you can't get your project funded by appealing to Bill Gates. Every minute of Bill Gates's time that Bill Gates makes available to philanthropists is a highly prized and fought-over resource. Every dollar of Gates's that he makes available to philanthropy is already highly fought over. You won't even get a chance to talk to him. Bill Gates is surrounded by a cloud of money, but you're very naive if you think that corresponds to him being surrounded by a cloud of free energy.

vi.

Since the idea of civilizational adequacy seems fairly useful and general, I initially wondered whether it might be a known idea (under some other name) in economics textbooks. But my friend Robin Hanson, a professional economist at an academic institution well-known for its economists, has written a lot of material that I see (from this theoretical perspective) as doing backwards reasoning from inadequacy to incentives.[18] If there were a widespread economic notion of adequacy that he were invoking, or standard models of academic incentives and academic inadequacy, I would expect him to cite them.

Now look at the above paragraph. Can you spot the two *implicit* arguments from adequacy?

The first sentence says, "To the extent that this way of generalizing the notion of an efficient market is conceptually useful, we should expect the field of economics to have been *adequate* to have already explored it in papers, and adequate at the task of disseminating the resulting knowledge to the point where my economist friends would be familiar with it."

The second and third sentences say, "If something like inadequacy analysis were already a well-known idea in economics, then I would expect my smart economist friend Robin Hanson to cite it. Even if Robin started out not knowing, I expect his other economist friends would tell him, or that one of the many economists reading his blog would comment on it. I expect the population of economists reading Robin's blog and papers to be *adequate* to the task of telling Robin about an existing field here, if one already existed."

Adequacy arguments are *ubiquitous*, and they're much more common in everyday reasoning than arguments about efficiency or exploitability.

---

[18]Robin often says things like, for example: "X doesn't use a prediction market, so X must not really care about accurate estimates." That is to say: "If system X were driven mainly by incentive Y, then it would have a Y-adequate equilibrium that would pick low-hanging fruit Z. But system X doesn't do Z, so X must not be driven mainly by incentive Y."

vii.

Returning to that business of stringing up 130 light bulbs around the house to treat my wife's Seasonal Affective Disorder:

Before I started, I tried to Google whether anyone had given "put up a ton of high-quality lights" a shot as a treatment for resistant SAD, and didn't find anything. Whereupon I shrugged, and started putting up LED bulbs.

Observing these choices of mine, we can infer that my inadequacy analysis was something like this: First, I did spend a fair amount of time Googling, and tried harder after the first search terms failed. This implies I started out thinking my civilization might have been adequate to think of the *more light* treatment and test it.

Then when I didn't find anything on Google, I went ahead and tested the idea myself, at considerable expense. I *didn't* assign such a high probability to "if this is a good idea, people will have tested it and propagated it to the point where I could find it" that in the absence of Google results, I could infer that the idea was bad.

I initially tried ordering the cheapest LED lights from Hong Kong that I could find on eBay. I didn't feel like I could rely on the US lighting market to equalize prices with Hong Kong, and so I wasn't confident that the premium price for US LED bulbs represented a quality difference. But when the cheap lights finally arrived from Hong Kong, they were dim, inefficient, and of visibly low color quality. So I decided to buy the more expensive US light bulbs for my next design iteration.

That is: I tried to save money based on a possible local inefficiency, but it turned out not to be inefficient, or at least not inefficient enough to be easily exploited by me. So I updated on that observation, discarded my previous belief, and changed my behavior.

Sometime after putting up the first 100 light bulbs or so, I was working on an earlier draft of this chapter and therefore reflecting more intensively on my process than I usually do. It occurred to me that sometimes the best academic content isn't online *and* that it might not be expensive to test that.

So I ordered a used $6 edited volume on Seasonal Affective Disorder, in case my Google-fu had failed me, hoping that a standard collection of papers would mention a light-intensity response curve that went past "standard lightbox."

Well, I've flipped through that volume, and so far it doesn't seem to contain any account of anyone having ever tried to cure resistant SAD using *more light*, either substantially higher-intensity or substantially higher-duration. I didn't find any table of response curves to light levels above 10,000 lux, or any experiments with all-day artificial light levels comparable to my apartment's roughly 2,000-lux luminance.

I say this to emphasize that I didn't lock myself into my attempted reasoning about adequacy when I realized it would cost $6 to perform a further observational check. And to be clear, ordering one book still isn't a strong check. It wouldn't surprise me in the least to learn that at least one researcher somewhere on Earth had tested the obvious thought of *more light* and published the response curve. But I'd also hesitate to bet at odds very far from 1:1 in either direction.

And the higher-intensity light therapy does seems to have mostly cured Brienne's SAD. It wasn't cheap, but it was cheaper than sending her to Chile for 4 months.

If *more light* really is a simple and effective treatment for a large percentage of otherwise resistant patients, is it truly plausible that no academic researcher out there has ever conducted the first investigation to cross my own mind? "Well, since the Sun itself clearly does work, let's try *more light* throughout the *whole house*—never mind these dinky lightboxes or 30-minute exposure times—and then just keep adding more light until it frickin' works." Is that really so non-obvious? With so many people around the world suffering from severe or subclinical SAD that resists lightboxes, with whole *countries* in the far North or South where the syndrome is common, could that experiment really have never been tried in a formal research setting?

On my model of the world? Sure.

Am I running out and trying to get a SAD researcher interested in my anecdotal data? No, because when something like this doesn't get done, there's usually a deeper reason than "nobody thought of it."

Even if nobody *did* think of it, that says something about a lack of incentives to be creative. If academics expected working solutions to SAD to be rewarded, there would already be a much larger body of literature on weird things researchers had tried, not just lightbox variant after lightbox variant. Inadequate systems tend systematically to be systemically unfixable; I don't know the exact details in this case, but there's probably something somewhere.

So I don't expect to get rich or famous, because I don't expect the system to be that exploitable in dollars or esteem, even though it *is* exploitable in personalized SAD treatments. Empirically, lots of people want money and acclaim, and base their short- and long-term career decisions around its pursuit; so achieving it in unusually large quantities shouldn't be as simple as having one bright idea. But there aren't large groups of competent people visibly organizing their day-to-day lives around producing outside-the-box new lightbox alternatives with the same intensity we can observe people organizing their lives around paying the bills, winning prestige or the acclaim of peers, etc.

People presumably *care* about curing SAD—if they could effortlessly push a button to instantly cure SAD, they would do so—but there's a big difference between "caring" and "caring enough to prioritize this over nearly everything else I care about," and it's the latter that would be needed for researchers to be willing to personally trade away non-small amounts of expected money or esteem for new treatment ideas.[19]

---

[19]Even the attention and awareness needed to explicitly consider the *option* of making such a tradeoff, in an environment where such tradeoffs aren't already normally made or discussed, is a limited resource. Researchers will not be motivated to take the time to *think about* pursuing more socially beneficial research strategies if they're *currently* pouring all their attention and strategic thinking into finding ways to achieve more of the other things they want in life.

In the case of Japan's monetary policy, it wasn't a coincidence that I couldn't get rich by understanding macroeconomics better than the Bank of Japan. Japanese asset markets shot up as soon as it became known that the Bank of Japan would create more money, without any need to wait and see—so it turns out that the markets also understood macroeconomics better than the Bank of Japan. Part of our civilization was being, in a certain sense, stupid: there were trillion-dollar bills lying around for the taking. But they weren't trillion-dollar bills that just anyone could walk over and pick up.

From the standpoint of a single agent like myself, that ecology didn't contain the particular kind of free energy that lots of other agents were competing to eat. I could be unusually right about macroeconomics compared to the PhD-bearing professionals at the Bank of Japan, but that weirdly low-hanging epistemic fruit wasn't a low-hanging financial fruit; I couldn't use the excess knowledge to easily get excess money deliverable the next day.

Where reward doesn't follow success, or where not everyone can individually pick up the reward, institutions and countries and whole civilizations can fail at what is usually imagined to be their tasks. And then it is very much easier to do better in some dimensions than to profit in others.

To state all of this more precisely: Suppose there is some space of strategies that you're competent enough to think up and execute on. *Inexploitability* has a single unit attached, like "$" or "effective SAD treatments," and says that you can't find a strategy in this space that knowably gets you much more of the resource in question than other agents. The kind of inexploitability I'm interested in typically arises when a large ecosystem of competing agents is genuinely trying to get the resource in question, and has access to strategies at least as good (for acquiring that resource) as the best options in your strategy space.

Conventional cynical economics doesn't require us to posit Machiavellian researchers who explicitly considered pursuing better strategies for treating SAD and decided against them for selfish reasons; they can just be too busy and distracted pursuing more obvious and immediate rewards, and never have a perceptible near-term incentive to even think very much about some other considerations.

Inadequacy with respect to a strategy space has two units attached, like "effective SAD treatments / research hours" or "QALYs / $," and says that there is some set of strategies a large ecosystem of agents could pursue that would convert the denominator unit into the numerator unit at some desired rate, but the agents are pursuing strategies that in fact result in a lower conversion rate. The kind of inadequacy I'm most interested in arises when many of the agents in the ecosystem would prefer that the conversion occur at the rate in question, but there's some systemic blockage preventing this from happening.

Systems tend to be inexploitable with respect to the resources that large ecosystems of competent agents are trying their hardest to pursue, like fame and money, regardless of how adequate or inadequate they are. And if there are other resources the agents aren't adequate at converting fame, money, etc. into at a widely desired rate, it will often be due to some systemic blockage. Insofar as agents have overlapping goals, it will therefore often be harder than it looks to find real instances of exploitability, and harder than it looks to outperform an inadequate equilibrium. But more local goals tend to overlap less: there isn't a large community of specialists specifically trying to improve my wife's well-being.

The academic and medical system probably isn't that easy to exploit in dollars or esteem, but so far it does look like maybe the system is exploitable in SAD innovations, due to being *inadequate* to the task of converting dollars, esteem, researcher hours, etc. into new SAD cures at a reasonable rate—inadequate, for example, at investigating some SAD cures that Randall Munroe would have considered obvious,[20] or at doing the basic investigative experiments that I would have considered obvious. And when the world is like that, it's possible to cure someone's crippling SAD by thinking carefully about the problem yourself, even if your civilization doesn't have a mainstream answer.

---

[20]See: https://what-if.xkcd.com/13/.

viii.

There's a whole lot more to be said about how to think about inadequate systems: common conceptual tools include Nash equilibria, commons problems, asymmetrical information, principal-agent problems, and more. There's also a whole lot more to be said about how *not* to think about inadequate systems.

In particular, if you relax your self-skepticism even slightly, it's trivial to come up with an *a priori* inadequacy argument for just about anything. Talk about "efficient markets" in any less than stellar forum, and you'll soon get half a dozen comments from people deriding the stupidity of hedge fund managers. And, yes, the financial system is broken in a lot of ways, but you still can't double your money trading S&P 500 stocks. "Find one thing to deride, conclude inadequacy" is not a good rule.

At the same time, lots of real-world social systems *do* have inadequate equilibria and it *is* important to be able to understand that, especially when we have clear observational evidence that this is the case. A blanket distrust of inadequacy arguments won't get us very far either.

This is one of those ideas where other cognitive skills are required to use it correctly, and you can shoot off your own foot by thinking wrongly. So if you've read this far, it's probably a good idea to keep reading.

3. Moloch's Toolbox

There's a toolbox of reusable concepts for analyzing systems I would call "inadequate"—the causes of civilizational failure, *some* of which correspond to local opportunities to do better yourself. I shall, somewhat arbitrarily, sort these concepts into three larger categories:

1. Decisionmakers who are not beneficiaries;

2. Asymmetric information;

and above all,

3. Nash equilibria that aren't even the best Nash equilibrium, let alone Pareto-optimal.

In other words:

1. Cases where the decision lies in the hands of people who would gain little personally, or lose out personally, if they did what was necessary to help someone else;

2. Cases where decision-makers can't reliably learn the information they need to make decisions, even though someone else has that information; and

3. Systems that are broken in multiple places so that no one actor can make them better, even though, in principle, some magically *coordinated* action could move to a new stable state.

I will then play fast and loose with these concepts in order to fit the entire Taxonomy of Failure inside them.

For example, "irrationality in the form of cognitive biases" wouldn't *obviously* fit into any of these categories, but I'm going to shove it inside "asymmetric information" via a clever sleight-of-hand. Ready? Here goes:

If *nobody* can detect a cognitive bias in particular cases, then from our perspective we can't really call it a "civilizational inadequacy" or "failure to pluck a low-hanging fruit." We shouldn't even be able to see it ourselves. So, on the contrary, let's suppose that you and some other people can indeed detect a cognitive bias that's screwing up civilizational decisionmaking.

Then why don't you just walk up to the decision-maker and *tell* them about the bias? Because they wouldn't have any way of knowing to trust *you* rather than the other five hundred people trying to influence their decisions? Well, in that case, you're holding information that they can't learn from you! So that's an "asymmetric information problem," in much the same way that it's an asymmetric information problem when you're trying to sell a used car and *you* know it doesn't have any mechanical problems, but you have no way of reliably conveying this knowledge to the buyer because for all they know you could be lying.

That argument is a bit silly, but so is the notion of trying to fit the whole Scroll of Woe into three supercategories. And if I named more than three supercategories, you wouldn't be able to remember them due to computational limitations (which aren't on the list anywhere, and I'm not going to add them).

i. For want of docosahexaenoic acids, a baby was lost

My discussion of modest epistemology in Chapter 1 might have given the impression that I think of modesty mostly as a certain set of high-level beliefs: beliefs about how best to combat cognitive bias, about how individual competencies stack up against group-level competencies, and so on. But I predict that many of this book's readers have high-level beliefs similar to those I outlined in Chapter 2, while employing a reasoning style that is really a special case of modest epistemology; and I think that this reasoning style is causing them substantial harm.

As reasoning styles, modest epistemology and inadequacy analysis depend on a mix of explicit principles and implicit mental habits. In inadequacy analysis, it's one thing to recognize in the abstract that we live in a world rife with systemic inefficiencies, and quite another to naturally *perceive* systems that way in daily life. So my goal here won't be to unkindly stick the label "inadequate" to a black box containing the world; it will be to say something about how the relevant systems actually operate.

For our central example, we'll be using the United States medical system, which is, so far as I know, the most broken system *that still works* ever recorded in human history. If you were reading about something in 19th-century France which was as broken as US healthcare, you wouldn't expect to find that it went on working when overloaded with a sufficiently vast amount of money. You would expect it to just not work at all.

In previous years, I would use the case of central-line infections as my go-to example of medical inadequacy. Central-line infections, in the US alone, killed 60,000 patients per year, and infected an additional 200,000 patients at an average treatment cost of $50,000/patient.

Central-line infections were also known to decrease by 50% or more if you enforced a five-item checklist that included items like "wash your hands before touching the line."

Robin Hanson has old *Overcoming Bias* blog posts on that untaken, low-hanging fruit. But I discovered while re-Googling in 2015 that wider adoption of hand-washing and similar precautions are now finally beginning to occur, after many years—with an associated 43% *nationwide* decrease in central-line infections. After *partial* adoption.[21]

---

[21] Carl Shulman notes that the Affordable Care Act linked federal payments to hospitals with reducing central-line infections (https://www.washington-post.com/news/wonk/wp/2013/05/31/the-cost-curve-is-bending-does-obamacare-deserve-the-credit/), which was probably a factor in the change.

So my new example is infants suffering liver damage, brain damage, and death in a way that's even easier to solve, by changing the lipid distribution of parenteral nutrition to match the proportions in breast milk.

Background: Some babies have digestion problems that require direct intravenous feeding. Long ago, somebody created a hospital formula for this intravenous feeding that matched the distribution of "fat," "protein," and "carbohydrate" in breast milk.

Just like "protein" comes in different amino acids, some of which the body can't make on its own and some of which it can, what early doctors used to think of as "fat" actually breaks down into metabolically distinct elements like short-chain triglycerides, medium-chain triglycerides, saturated fat, and omega-6, omega-9, and the famous "omega-3." "Omega-3" is actually several different lipids in its own right; vegetable oils with "omega-3" usually just contain alpha-linolenic acids, which can only be inefficiently converted to ecosapentaenoic acids, which are then even more inefficiently converted to docosahexaenoic acids, which are the actual key structural components in the body. This conversion pathway is rate-limited by a process that also converts omega-6, so too much omega-6 can prevent you from processing ALA into DHA even if you're getting ALA.

So what happens if your infant nutrition was initially designed based on the concept of "fat" as a natural category, and all the "fat" in the mix comes from soybean oil?

From a popular book by Jaminet and Jaminet:

> Some babies are born with "short bowel syndrome" and need to be given parenteral nutrition, or nutrition delivered intravenously directly to the blood, until their digestive tracts grow and heal. Since 1961, parenteral nutrition has used soybean oil as its source of fat.[6] And for decades, babies on parenteral nutrition have suffered devastating liver and brain damage. The death rate on soybean oil is 30 percent by age four. [...]

In a clinical trial, of forty-two babies given fish oil [after they had already developed liver damage on soybean oil], three died and one required a liver transplant; of forty-nine given soybean oil, twelve died and six required a liver transplant.[8] The death-or-liver-transplant rate was reduced from 37 percent with soybean oil to 9 percent with fish oil.[22]

When Jaminet and Jaminet wrote the above, in 2012, there was a single hospital in the United States that could provide correctly formulated parenteral nutrition, namely the Boston Children's Hospital; nowhere else. This formulation was illegal to sell across state lines.

A few years *after* the Boston Children's Hospital developed their formula—keeping in mind the heap of dead babies continuing to pile up in the meanwhile—there developed a shortage of "certified lipids" (FDA-approved "fat" for adding to parenteral nutrition). For a year or two, the parenteral nutrition contained *no fat at all* which is *worse* and can kill *adults*.

You see, although there's nothing special about the soybean oil in parenteral nutrition, there was only one US manufacturer approved to add it, and that manufacturer left the market, so…

As of 2015, the state of affairs was as follows: The FDA eventually solved the problem with the shortage of US-certified lipids, by… allowing US hospitals to import parenteral nutrition bags from Europe. And it only took them two years' worth of dead patients to figure that out!

As of 2016, if your baby has short bowel syndrome, and has *already* ended up with liver damage, and either you or your doctor is lucky enough to know what's wrong and how to fix it, your doctor can apply for a special permit

---

[22] Around a thousand infants are born with short bowel syndrome per year in the United States, of whom two-thirds develop parenteral nutrition-associated liver disease (http://journals.sagepub.com/doi/abs/10.1177/0148607114527772). See https://www.nature.com/jp/journal/v31/n1s/full/jp2010182a.html for a 2011 review of the academic literature, and http://rockcenter.nbcnews.com/_news/2013/06/07/18833434-drug-treatment-omegaven-that-could-save-infants-lives-not-yet-approved-by-fda and https://www.dailyherald.com/article/20110118/news/701199905/ for news coverage.

to use a non-FDA-approved substance for your child on an emergency basis. After this, you can buy Omegaven and hope that it cures your baby and that there isn't too much permanent damage and that it's not already too late.

This is an improvement over the prior situation, where the non-poisonous formulation was illegal to sell across state lines under any circumstances, but it's still not *good* by any stretch of the imagination.

Now imagine trying to explain to a visitor from a relatively well-functioning world just why it is that your civilization has killed a bunch of babies and subjected other babies to pointless brain damage.

"It's not that we're *evil*," you say helplessly, "it's that... well, you see, it's not that anyone *wanted* to kill those babies, it's just the way the System ended up, somehow..."

ii. Asymmetric information and lemons problems

Three people have gathered in a blank white space:

- The **Visitor** from a Better World;

- **Simplicio**, who is attending a major university but hasn't taken under-graduate economics;

- **Cecie**, the Conventional Cynical Economist.

The Visitor speaks first.

VISITOR: So I've listened to you explain about babies suffering death and brain damage from parenteral nutrition built on soybean oil. I have several questions here, but I'll start with the most obvious one.

CECIE: Go ahead.

VISITOR: Why aren't there riots?

SIMPLICIO: The first thing you have to understand, Visitor, is that the folk in this world are hypocrites, cowards, psychopaths, and sheep.

I mean, *I* certainly care about the the lives of newborn children. Hearing about their plight certainly makes *me* want to do something about it. When I see the problem continuing in spite of that, I can only conclude that other people *don't* feel the level of moral indignation that I feel when staring at a heap of dead babies.

CECIE: I don't think that hypothesis is needed, Simplicio. As a start, Visitor, you have to realize that the picture I've shown you is not widely known. Maybe 10% of the population, at most, is walking around with the prior belief that the FDA in general is killing people; our government runs on majority rule and the 10% can't unilaterally defy it.[23] Maybe 0.1% of that 10% know that omega-3 ALA is converted into omega-3 DHA via a metabolic pathway that competes with omega-6. And then most of those aren't aware of what's happening to babies right now.

VISITOR: Pointing to that state of ignorance is hardly a sufficient explanation! If a theater is on fire and only one person knows it, they yell "Fire!" and then more people know it. People from my civilization would scream "Babies are dying over here!" and other people from my civilization would whip around their heads and look.

SIMPLICIO: Our world's cowards and sheep would hear that and think that it's (a) somebody else's problem and (b) all part of the plan.

CECIE: In our world, Visitor, we have an economic phenomenon sometimes called the lemons problem. Suppose you want to sell a used car, and I'm looking for a car to buy. From my perspective, I have to worry that your car might be a "lemon"—that it has a serious mechanical problem that doesn't appear every time you start the car, and is difficult or impossible to

---

[23] See Tabarrok's "Assessing the FDA via the Anomaly of Off-Label Drug Prescribing," which cites the widespread practice of off-label prescription as evidence that the FDA's efficacy trial requirements are unnecessary (http://www.independent.org/pdf/tir/tir_05_1_tabarrok.pdf).

fix. Now, *you* know that your car isn't a lemon. But if I ask you, "Hey, is this car a lemon?" and you answer "No," I can't trust your answer, because you're incentivized to answer "No" either way. Hearing you say "No" isn't much Bayesian evidence. *Asymmetric information* conditions can persist even in cases where, like an honest seller meeting an honest buyer, both parties have strong incentives for accurate information to be conveyed.

A further problem is that if the fair value of a non-lemon car is $10,000, and the possibility that your car is a lemon causes me to only be willing to pay you $8,000, you might refuse to sell your car. So the honest sellers with reliable cars start to leave the market, which further shifts upward the probability that any given car for sale is a lemon, which makes me less willing to pay for a used car, which incentivizes more honest sellers to leave the market, and so on.

VISITOR: What does the lemons problem have to do with your world's inability to pass around information about dead babies?

CECIE: In our world, there are a lot of people screaming, "Pay attention to this thing I'm indignant about over here!" In fact, there are enough people screaming that there's an inexploitable market in indignation. The dead-babies problem can't compete in that market; there's no free energy left for it to eat, and it doesn't have an optimal indignation profile. There's no single individual villain. The business about competing omega-3 and omega-6 metabolic pathways is something that only a fraction of people would understand on a visceral level; and even if those people posted it to their Facebook walls, most of their readers wouldn't understand and repost, so the dead-babies problem has relatively little virality. Being indignant about this particular thing doesn't signal your moral superiority to anyone else in particular, so it's not viscerally enjoyable to engage in the indignation. As for adding a further scream, "But wait, this matter *really is* important!", that's the part subject to the lemons problem. Even people who honestly know about a fixable case of dead babies can't emit a *trustworthy* request for attention.

SIMPLICIO: You're saying that people won't listen even if I sound *really* indignant about this? That's an outrage!

CECIE: By this point in our civilization's development, many honest buyers and sellers have left the indignation market entirely; and what's left behind is not, on average, good.

VISITOR: Your reply contains so many surprising postulates of weird civilizational dysfunction, I hardly know what to ask about next. So instead I'll try to explain how my world works, and you can explain to me why your world doesn't work that way.

CECIE: Sounds reasonable.

iii. Academic incentives and beneficiaries

VISITOR: To start with, in my world, we have these people called "scientists" who verify claims experimentally, and other people trust the "scientists." So if our "scientists" say that a certain formula seems to be killing babies, this would provoke general indignation without every single listener needing to study docohexa-whatever acids.

SIMPLICIO: Alas, our so-called scientists are just pawns of the same medical-industrial complex that profits from killing babies.

CECIE: I'm afraid, Visitor, that although there are strong prior reasons to expect too much omega-6 and no omega-3 to be very bad for an infant baby, and there are now a few dozen small-scale studies which seem to match that prediction, this matter hasn't had the massive study that would begin to produce confident scientific agreement—

VISITOR: You'd better not be pointing to *that* as an exogenous fact that explains your civilization's problem! See, on my planet, if somebody points to *strong prior suspicion* combined with *confirming pilot studies* saying that something is killing innocent babies and is fixable, and the pilot studies are not considered sufficient evidence to settle the issue, our people would *do more studies* and wouldn't just go on blindly feeding the babies poison in the meantime. Our scientists would all agree on *that*!

CECIE: But people loudly agreeing on something, by itself, accomplishes nothing. It's all well and good for everyone to agree in principle that larger studies ought to be done; but in your world, who actually does the big study, and why do they do it?

VISITOR: Two subclasses within the profession of "scientist" are *suggesters*, whose piloting studies provide the initial suspicions of effects, and *replicators* whose job it is to confirm the result and nail things down solidly—the exact effect size and so on. When an important suggestive result arises, two replicators step forward to confirm it and nail down the exact conditions for producing it, being forbidden upon their honor to communicate with each other until they submit their findings. If both replicators agree on the particulars, that completes the discovery. The three funding bodies that sustained the suggester and the dual replicators would receive the three places of honor in the announcement. Do I need to explain how part of the function of any civilized society is to appropriately reward those who contribute to the public good?

CECIE: Well, that's not how things work on Earth. Our world gives almost all the public credit and fame to the *discoverer*, as the initial suggester is called among us. Our scientists often *say* that replication is important, but our most prestigious journals won't publish mere replications; nor do the history books remember them. The outcome is a lot of small studies that have just enough subjects to obtain "statistically significant" results—

VISITOR: ... What? Probability is quantitative, not qualitative. There's no such thing as a "significant" or "insignificant" likelihood ratio—

CECIE: *Anyway*, while it might be good if larger studies were done, *the decisionmaker is not the beneficiary*—the people who did the extra work of a larger study, and funded the extra work of a larger study, would not receive fame and fortune thereby.

VISITOR: I must be missing something basic here. You do have multiple studies, right? When you have multiple bodies of data, you can multiply the likelihood functions from the studies' respective data to the hypotheses to obtain the meaning of the *combined* evidence—the likelihood function from *all* the data to the hypotheses.[24]

CECIE: I'm afraid you can't do that on Earth.

VISITOR: ... Of course you can. It's a *mathematical theorem*. You can't possibly tell me *that* differs between our universes!

Yes, there are pitfalls for the especially careless. Sometimes studies end up being conducted under different circumstances, with the result that the naively computed likelihood functions don't have uniform relations to the hypotheses under consideration. In that case, blindly multiplying will give you a likelihood function that's nearly zero everywhere. But, I mean, if you just look at all the likelihood functions, it's pretty obvious when some of them are pointing in different directions and then you can *investigate that divergence.*

Either it makes sense to multiply all the likelihood functions and get out one massive evidential pointer, or else you *don't* get a sensible result when you multiply them and then you know something's wrong with your methods—

CECIE: I'm afraid our scientific community doesn't run on your world's statistical methods. You see, during the first half of the twentieth century, it became conventional to measure something called "*p*-values" which imposed a qualitative distinction between "successful" and "unsuccessful" experiments—

VISITOR: *That is still not an explanation.* Why not *change* the way you do things?

CECIE: Because somebody who tried using unconventional statistical methods, even if they were better statistical methods, wouldn't be able to publish their papers in the most prestigious journals. And then they

---

[24] See the "Report Likelihoods, Not *p*-Values" FAQ (https://arbital.com/p/likelihoods_not_pvalues/?l=505), or, in dialogue form: "Likelihood Functions, *p*-Values, and the Replication Crisis" (https://arbital.com/p/likelihoods_not_pvalues/?l=4xx).

wouldn't get hired. It's similar to the way that the most prestigious journals don't publish mere replications, only discoveries, so people focus on making discoveries instead of replications.

VISITOR: Why would anyone *pay attention* to journals like that?

CECIE: Because university hiring departments care a lot about whether you've published in prestigious journals.

VISITOR: No, I mean… how did these journals end up prestigious in the first place? *Why* do university hiring departments pay attention to them?

SIMPLICIO: Why *would* university hiring departments care about real science? Shouldn't it be you who has to explain why some lifeless cog of the military-industrial complex would care about anything except grant money?

CECIE: Okay… you're digging pretty deep here. I think I need to back up and try to explain things on a more basic level.

VISITOR: Indeed, I think you should. So far, every time I've asked you why someone is acting insane, you've claimed that it's secretly a sane response to someone else acting insane. Where does this process bottom out?

iv. Two-factor markets and signaling equilibria

CECIE: Let me try to identify a first step on which insanity can emerge from non-insanity. Universities pay attention to prestigious journals because of a *signaling equilibrium*, which, in our taxonomy, is a kind of bad Nash equilibrium that no single actor can defy unilaterally.

In your terms, it involves a sticky, stable equilibrium of *everyone* acting insane in a way that's secretly a sane response to everyone else acting insane.

VISITOR: Go on.

CECIE: First, let me explain the idea of what Eliezer has nicknamed a "two-factor market." Two-factor markets are a conceptually simpler case that will help us later understand signaling equilibria.

In our world there's a crude site for classified ads, called Craigslist. Craigslist doesn't contain any way of rating users, the way that eBay lets buyers and sellers rate each other, or that Airbnb lets renters and landlords rate each other.

Suppose you wanted to set up a version of Craigslist that let people rate each other. Would you be able to compete with Craigslist?

The answer is that even if this innovation is in fact a good one, competing with Craigslist would be far more difficult than it sounds, because Craigslist is sustained by a two-factor market. The sellers go where there are the most buyers; the buyers go where they expect to find sellers. When you launch your new site, no buyers will want to go there because there are no sellers, and no sellers will want to go there because there are no buyers. Craigslist initially broke into this market by targeting San Francisco particularly, and spending marketing effort to assemble the San Francisco buyers and sellers into the same place. But that would be harder to do for a later startup, because now the people it's targeting are already using Craigslist.

SIMPLICIO: Those sheep! Just mindlessly doing whatever their incentives tell them to!

CECIE: We can imagine that there's a better technology than Craigslist, called Danslist, such that everyone using Craigslist would be better off if they all switched to Danslist simultaneously. But if just one buyer or just one seller is the first to go to Danslist, they find an empty parking lot. In conventional cynical economics, we'd say that this is a *coordination problem*—

SIMPLICIO: A coordination problem? What do you mean by that?

CECIE: Backing up a bit: A "Nash equilibrium" is what happens when everyone makes their best move, given that all the other players are making their best moves from that Nash equilibrium—everyone goes to Craigslist, because that's their individually best move *given* that everyone else is going to Craigslist. A "Pareto optimum" is any situation where it's impossible to make every actor better off simultaneously, like "Cooperate/Cooperate" in the Prisoner's Dilemma—there's no alternative outcome to Cooperate/Cooperate that makes *both* agents better off. The Prisoner's Dilemma is a coordination problem because the sole Nash equilibrium of Defect/Defect isn't Pareto-optimal; there's an outcome, Cooperate/Cooperate, that both players prefer, but aren't reaching.

SIMPLICIO: How stupid of them!

CECIE: No, it's... ah, never mind. Anyway, the *frustrating* parts of civilization are the times when you're stuck in a Nash equilibrium that's Pareto-inferior *to other Nash equilibria*. I mean, it's not surprising that humans have trouble getting to non-Nash optima like "both sides cooperate in the Prisoner's Dilemma without any other means of enforcement or verification." What makes an equilibrium *inadequate*, a fruit that seems to hang tantalizingly low and yet somehow our civilization isn't plucking, is when there's a better *stable* state and we haven't reached it.

VISITOR: Indeed. Moving from bad equilibria to better equilibria is the whole point of having a civilization in the first place.

CECIE: Being stuck in an inferior Nash equilibrium is how I'd describe the frustrating aspect of the two-factor market of buyers and sellers that can't switch from Craigslist to Danslist. The scenario where everyone is using Danslist *would* be a stable Nash equilibrium, and a *better* Nash equilibrium. We just can't get there from here. There's no one actor who is behaving foolishly; all the individuals are responding strategically to their incentives. It's only the larger system that behaves "foolishly." I'm not aware of a standard term for this situation, so I'll call it an "inferior equilibrium."

SIMPLICIO: Why do you care what academics call it? Why not just use the *best* phrase?

CECIE: The terminology "inferior equilibrium" would be fine if everyone else were already using that terminology. Mostly I want to use the same phrase that everyone else uses, even if it's not the best phrase.

SIMPLICIO: Regardless, I'm not seeing what the grand obstacle is to people solving these problems by, you know, *coordinating*. If people would just act in unity, so much could be done!

I feel like you're placing too much blame on system-level issues, Cecie, when the simpler hypothesis is just that the people *in* the system are terrible: bad at thinking, bad at caring, bad at coordinating. You claim to be a "cynic," but your whole world-view sounds rose-tinted to me.

VISITOR: Even in my world, Simplicio, coordination isn't as simple as everyone jumping simultaneously every time one person shouts "Jump!" For coordinated action to be successful, you need to trust the institution that says what the action should be, and a *majority* of people have to trust that institution, and they have to *know* that other people trust the institution, so that everyone *expects* the coordinated action to occur at the critical time, so that it makes sense for them to act too.

That's why we have policy prediction markets and... there doesn't seem to be a word in your language for the *timed-collective-action-threshold-conditional-commitment*... hold on, this cultural translator isn't making any sense. "Kickstarter"? You have the key concept, but you use it mainly for making video games?

CECIE: I'll now introduce the concept of a *signaling equilibrium*.

To paraphrase a commenter on *Slate Star Codex*: suppose that there's a magical tower that only people with IQs of at least 100 and some amount of conscientiousness can enter, and this magical tower slices four years off your lifespan. The natural next thing that happens is that employers start to prefer prospective employees who have proved they can enter the tower, and employers offer these employees higher salaries, or even make entering the tower a condition of being employed at all.[25]

---

[25] From Schmidt and Hunter's "Select on Intelligence" (http://www.blackwellreference. com/public/tocnode?id=g9780631215066_chunk_g97806312150662): "Intelligence is the major determinant of job performance, and therefore hiring people based on intelligence leads to marked improvements in job performance." See also psychologist Stu-

VISITOR: Hold on. There *must* be less expensive ways of testing intelligence and conscientiousness than sacrificing four years of your lifespan to a magical tower.

CECIE: Let's not go into that right now. For now, just take as an exogenous fact that employers can't get all of the information they want by other channels.

VISITOR: But—

CECIE: Anyway: the natural next thing that happens is that employers start to demand that prospective employees show a certificate saying that they've been inside the tower. This makes *everyone* want to go to the tower, which enables somebody to set up a fence around the tower and charge hundreds of thousands of dollars to let people in.[26]

VISITOR: But—

art Ritchie's discussion of IQ in *Vox* (https://www.vox.com/2016/5/25/11683192/iq-testing-intelligence).

Software engineer Alyssa Vance adds:

> I'll note that, as far as I can tell, the informal consensus at least among the best-informed people in software is that hiring has tons of obvious irrationality even when there's definitely no external cause; see https://sockpuppet.org/blog/2015/03/06/the-hiring-post/ and https://danluu.com/programmer-moneyball/.

> In terms of Moloch's toolbox, the obvious reason for that is that interviewers are rarely judged on the quality of the people they accept, and when they are, certainly aren't paid more or less based on it. (Never mind the people they reject. "Nobody ever got fired because of the later performance of someone they turned down.") Their incentive, insofar as they have one, is to hire people who they'd most prefer to be on the same floor with all day long.

[26]Compare psychiatrist Scott Alexander's account, in "Against Tulip Subsidies" (https://slatestarcodex.com/2015/06/06/against-tulip-subsidies/):

> In America, aspiring doctors do four years of undergrad in whatever area they want (I did Philosophy), then four more years of medical school, for a total of eight years post-high school education. In Ireland, aspiring doctors go straight from high school to medical school and finish after five years.

CECIE: Now, fortunately, after Tower One is established and has been running for a while, somebody tries to set up a competing magical tower, Tower Two, that also drains four years of life but charges less money to enter.

VISITOR: … You're *solving the wrong problem.*

CECIE: Unfortunately, there's a subtle way in which this competing Tower Two is hampered by the same kind of lock-in that prevents a jump from Craigslist to Danslist. Initially, all of the smartest people headed to Tower One. Since Tower One had limited room, it started discriminating further among its entrants, only taking the ones that have IQs above the minimum,

---

I've done medicine in both America and Ireland. The doctors in both countries are about equally good. When Irish doctors take the American standardized tests, they usually do pretty well. Ireland is one of the approximately 100% of First World countries that gets better health outcomes than the United States. There's no evidence whatsoever that American doctors gain anything from those three extra years of undergrad. And why would they? Why is having a philosophy degree under my belt supposed to make me any better at medicine? […]

I'll make another confession. Ireland's medical school is five years as opposed to America's four because the Irish spend their first year teaching the basic sciences—biology, organic chemistry, physics, calculus. When I applied to medical school in Ireland, they offered me an accelerated four year program on the grounds that I had surely gotten all of those in my American undergraduate work. I hadn't. I read some books about them over the summer and did just fine.

Americans take eight years to become doctors. Irishmen can do it in four, and achieve the same result. Each year of higher education at a good school—let's say an Ivy, doctors don't study at Podunk Community College—costs about $50,000. So American medical students are paying an extra $200,000 for…what?

Remember, a modest amount of the current health care crisis is caused by doctors' crippling level of debt. Socially responsible doctors often consider less lucrative careers helping the needy, right up until the bill comes due from their education and they realize they have to make a lot of money right now. We took one look at that problem and said "You know, let's make doctors pay an extra $200,000 for no reason."

For a more general discussion of the evidence that college is chiefly a costly signal of pre-existing ability, rather than a mechanism for building skills and improving productivity, see Bryan Caplan's argument in "Is College Worth It?" (https://www.cato.org/events/college-worth-it), also summarized by Roger Barris (http://www.economicmanblog.com/2017/02/25/college-capital-or-signal/).

or who are good at athletics or have rich parents or something. So when Tower Two comes along, the employers still *prefer* employees from Tower One, which has a more famous reputation. So the smartest people still prefer to apply to Tower One, even though it costs more money. This stabilizes Tower One's reputation as being the place where the smartest people go.

In other words, the signaling equilibrium is a two-factor market in which the stable point, Tower One, is cemented in place by the individually best choices of two different parts of the system. Employers prefer Tower One because it's where the smartest people go. Smart employees prefer Tower One because employers will pay them more for going there. If you try dissenting from the system unilaterally, without everyone switching at the same time, then as an employer you end up hiring the less-qualified people from Tower Two, or as an employee, you end up with lower salary offers after you go to Tower Two. So the system is stable as a matter of individual incentives, and stays in place. If you try to set up a cheaper alternative to the whole Tower system, the *default* thing that happens to you is that people who couldn't handle the Towers try to go through your new system, and it acquires a reputation for non-prestigious weirdness and incompetence.

VISITOR: This all just seems so weird and complicated. I'm skeptical that this scenario with the magical towers could happen in real life.

SIMPLICIO: I agree that trying to build a cheaper Tower Two is solving the wrong problem. The interior of Tower One boasts some truly exquisite architecture and decor. It just makes sense that *someone* should pay a lot to allow people entry to Tower One. What we really need is for the government to subsidize the entry fees on Tower One, so that more people can fit inside.

CECIE: Consider a simpler example: Velcro is a system for fastening shoes that is, for at least some people and circumstances, better than shoelaces. It's easier to adjust three separate Velcro straps then it is to keep your shoelaces perfectly adjusted at all loops, it's faster to do and undo, et cetera, and not everyone is running at high speeds that call for perfectly adjusted running shoes. But when Velcro was introduced, the earliest people to adopt Velcro were those who had the most trouble tying their shoelaces—very young children and the elderly. So Velcro became associated with kids and old people, and thus unforgivably *unfashionable*, regardless of whether it would have been better than shoelaces in some adult applications as well.

VISITOR: I take it you didn't have the stern and upright leaders, what we call the Serious People, who could set an example by donning Velcro shoes themselves?

SIMPLICIO & CECIE: (*in unison*) No.

VISITOR: I see.

CECIE: Now consider the system of scientific journals that we were originally talking about. Some journals are prestigious. So university hiring committees pay the most attention to publications in that journal. So people with the best, most interesting-looking publications try to send them to that journal. So if a university hiring committee paid an equal amount of attention to publications in lower-prestige journals, they'd end up granting tenure to less prestigious people. Thus, the whole system is a stable equilibrium that nobody can unilaterally defy except at cost to themselves.

VISITOR: I'm still skeptical. Doesn't your parable of the magical tower suggest that, if that's actually true, somebody ought to rope off the journals too and charge insane amounts of money?

CECIE: Yes, and that's exactly what happened. Elsevier and a few other profiteers grabbed the most prestigious journals and started jacking up the access costs. They contributed almost nothing—even the peer review and editing was done by unpaid volunteers. Elsevier just charged more and more money and sat back. This is standardly called *rent-seeking*. In a few cases, the scientists were able to kickstart a coordinated move where the entire editing board would resign, start a new journal, and everybody in the field would submit to the new journal instead. But since our scientists don't have recognized kickstarting customs, or any software support for them, it isn't easy to pull that off. Most of the big-name journals that Elsevier has captured are still big names, still getting prestigious submissions, and still capturing big-money rents.

VISITOR: Well, I guess I understand why my cultural translator keeps putting air quotes around Earth's version of "science." The whole idea of science, as I understand the concept, is that everything has to be in the open for anyone to verify. Science is the part of humanity's knowledge that everyone can potentially learn about and reproduce themselves. You can't *charge money* in order for people to read your experimental results, or you lose the "everyone can access and verify your claims" property that distinguishes science from other kinds of information.

CECIE: Oh, rest assured that scientists aren't seeing any of this money. It all goes to the third-party journal owners.

SIMPLICIO: And this isn't just scientists being stupid?

CECIE: No stupider than you are for going to college. It's hard to beat *signaling equilibria*—because they're "multi-factor markets"—which are special cases of *coordination problems* that create "inferior Nash equilibria"—which are so stuck in place that market controllers can *seek rent* on the value generated by captive participants.

SIMPLICIO: Weren't we talking about dead babies at some point?

CECIE: Yes, we were. I was explaining how our system allocated too much credit to discoverers and not enough credit to replicators, and the only socially acceptable statistics couldn't aggregate small-scale trials in a way regarded as reliable. The Visitor asked me why the system was like that. I pointed to journals that published a particular kind of paper. The Visitor asked me why anyone paid attention to those journals in the first place. I explained about signaling equilibria, and that's where we are now.

VISITOR: I can't say that I feel enlightened at the end of walking through all that. There must be *particular* scientists on the editorial boards who choose not to demand replications and who forbid multiplying likelihood ratios. Why are those particular scientists doing the non-sensible thing?

CECIE: Because people in the general field wouldn't cite nonstandard papers, so if the editors demanded nonstandard papers, the journal's publication factor would decrease.

VISITOR: Why don't the journal editors start by demanding that paper submitters *cite* dual replications as well as initial suggestions?

CECIE: Because that would be a weird unconventional demand, which might lead people with high-prestige results to submit those results to other journals instead. Fundamentally, you're asking why scientists on Earth don't adopt certain new customs that you think would be for the good of everyone. And the answer is that there's this big, multi-factor system that nobody can dissent from unilaterally, and that people have a *lot* of trouble coordinating to change. That's true even when there are forces like Elsevier that are being *blatant* about ripping everyone off. Implementing your proposed cultural shift to "suggesters" and "replicators," or using likelihood functions, would be significantly *harder* than everyone just simultaneously ceasing to deal with Elsevier, since the case for it would be less obvious and would provoke more disagreement. All that we can manage is to make incremental shifts toward funding more replication and asking more for study preregistration.

To sum up, academic science is embedded in a big enough system with enough separate decisionmakers creating incentives for other decisionmakers that it almost always takes the path of least resistance. The system isn't in the *best* Nash equilibrium because nobody has the power to look over the system and choose *good* Nash equilibria. It's just in *a* Nash equilibrium that it wandered into, which includes statistical methods that were invented in the first half of the 20th century and editors not demanding that people cite replications.

VISITOR: I see. And that's why nobody in your world has multiplied the likelihood functions, or done a large-enough single study, or otherwise done *whatever it would take* to convince whoever needs to be convinced about the effects of feeding infants soybean oil.

CECIE: It's one of the reasons. A large study would also be very *expensive* because of extreme paperwork requirements, generated by other systemic failures I haven't gotten around to talking about yet—[27]

VISITOR: How does anything get done *ever*, in your world?

CECIE: —and when it comes to funding or carrying out that bigger study, *the decisionmaker would not significantly benefit* under the current system, which is held in place by *coordination problems*. And that's why people who already have a background grasp of lipid metabolic pathways have *asymmetric information* about what is worth becoming indignant about.

v. Total market failures

VISITOR: Even granting the things you've said already, I don't feel like I've been told enough to understand why your society is killing babies.

CECIE: Well, *no*. Not yet. The lack of incentive to do a large-scale convincing study is only *one* thing that went wrong inside *one* part of the system. There's a lot *more* broken than just that—which is why effective altruists shouldn't be running out and trying to fund a big replication study for Omegaven, because that by itself wouldn't fix things.

VISITOR: Okay, suppose there *had* been a large enough study to satisfy your world's take on "scientists." What *else* would likely go wrong after that?

CECIE: Several things. For example, doctors wouldn't necessarily be aware of the experimental results.

VISITOR: Hold on, I think my cultural translator is broken. You used that word "doctor" and my translator spit out a long sequence of words for Examiner plus Diagnostician plus Treatment Planner plus Surgeon plus Outcome Evaluator plus Student Trainer plus Business Manager. Maybe

---

[27] See, e.g., Scott Alexander's "My IRB Nightmare" (http://slatestar-codex.com/2017/08/29/my-irb-nightmare/).

it's stuck and spitting out the names of all the professions associated with medicine.

CECIE: So, in your world, if there is a dual replication of results on Omegaven versus soybean oil, how does that end up changing the actual patient treatments?

VISITOR: By informing the Treatment Planners who specialize in infant ailments that required parenteral nutrition, of course. The discovery would appear inside the "parenteral nutrition" pages in the Earthweb and show up in the feeds of everyone subscribed to that page. The statistics would appear inside the Treatment Planner's decision-support software. And if all of those broke for some reason, every Treatment Planner for infant ailments that required parenteral nutrition would just use chatrooms. And anyone who ignored the chatrooms would have worse patient outcome ratings, and would lose status relative to Treatment Planners who were more attentive.

CECIE: It sounds like "Treatment Planners" in your world are much more specialized than doctors in this world. I suppose they're also selected specifically for talent at... cost-benefit analysis and decision theory, or something along those lines? And then they focus their learning on particular diseases for which they are Treatment Planners? And somebody else tracks their outcomes?

VISITOR: Of course. I'm... almost afraid to ask, but how do they do it in your world?

CECIE: Your translator wasn't broken. In our world, "doctors" are supposed to examine patients for symptoms, diagnose especially complicated or obscure ailments using their encyclopedic knowledge and their keen grasp of Bayesian inference, plan the patient's treatment by weighing the costs and benefits of the latest treatments, execute the treatments using their keen dexterity and reliable stamina, evaluate for themselves how well that went, train students to do it too, and in many cases, *also* oversee the small business that bills the patients and markets itself. So "doctors" have to be selected for all of those talents simultaneously, and then split their training, experience, and attention between them.

VISITOR: *Why* in the name of—

CECIE: Oh, and before they go to medical school, we usually send them off to get a four-year degree in philosophy first or something, just because.

I don't know if there's a standard name for this phenomenon, but we can call it "failure of professional specialization." It also appears when, for example, a lawyer has to learn calculus in order to graduate college, even though their job doesn't require any calculus.

VISITOR: Why. Why. Why why why—

CECIE: I'm not sure. I suspect the origin has something to do with status— like, a high-status person can do all things at once, so it's insulting and lowers status to suggest that an esteemed and respectable Doctor should only practice one surgical operation and get very good at it. And once you yourself have spent twelve years being trained under the current system, you won't be happy about the proposal to replace it with two years of much more specialized training. Once you've been through a painful initiation ritual and rationalized its necessity, you'll hate to see anyone else going through a less painful one. Not to mention that you won't be happy about the competition against your own human capital, by a cheaper and better form of human capital—and after the sunk cost in pain and time that you endured to build human capital under the old system…

VISITOR: Do they not have markets on your planet? Because on my planet, when you manufacture your product in a crazy, elaborate, expensive way that produces an inferior product, someone else will come along and rationalize the process and take away your customers.

CECIE: We have markets, but there's this unfortunate thing called "regula-tory capture," of which one kind is "occupational licensing."

As an example, it used to be that chairs were carefully hand-crafted one at the time by carpenters who had to undergo a lengthy apprenticeship, and indeed, they didn't like it when factories came along staffed by people who specialized in just carving a single kind of arm. But the factory-made chairs were vastly cheaper and most of the people who insisted on sticking to handcrafts soon went out of business.

Now imagine: What if the chair-makers had been extremely respectable—had already possessed very high status? What if their profession had an element of danger? What if they'd managed to frighten everyone about the dangers of improperly made chairs that might dump people on the ground and snap their necks?

VISITOR: Okay, yes, we used to have Serious People who would go around and certify the making of some medicines where somebody might be tempted to cheat and use inferior ingredients. But that was before *computers* and *outcome statistics* and *online ratings*.

CECIE: And on our planet, Uber and Lyft are currently fighting it out with taxi companies and their pet regulators after exactly that development. But suppose the whole system was set up before the existence of online ratings. Then the carpenters might have managed to introduce occupational licensing on who could be a carpenter. So if you tried to set up a factory, your factory workers would have needed to go through the traditional carpentry apprenticeship that covered every part of every kind of furniture, before they were legally allowed to come to your factory and specialize in carving just one kind of chair-arm. And then your factory would also need a ton of permits to sell its furniture, and would need to inveigle orders from a handful of resellers who were licensed to buy and resell furniture at a fixed margin. That small, insular group of resellers might not benefit *literally personally*—in their own personal salary—from buying from your cheaper factory system. And so it would go.

VISITOR: But why would the legislators go along with that?

CECIE: Because the carpenters would have a big, concentrated incentive to figure out how to make legislators do it—maybe by hiring very persuasive people, or by subtle bribery, or by not-so-subtle bribery.

Insofar as occupational licensing works to the benefit of professionals at the expense of consumers, occupational licensing represents a kind of regulatory capture, which happens when a few regulatees have a much more concentrated incentive to affect the regulation process. Regulatory capture in turn is a kind of commons problem, since every citizen shares the benefits of non-captured regulation, but no individual citizen has a sufficient incentive to unilaterally spend their life attending to that particular regulatory problem. So occupational licensing is regulatory capture is a commons problem is a coordination problem.

VISITOR: Then... the upshot is that it's impossible for your country to *test* a functional hospital design *in the first place?* The reformers can't win the competition because they're not legally allowed to try?

CECIE: But of course. Though in this case, if you did manage to set up a test hospital working along more reasonable lines, you still wouldn't be able to advertise your better results relative to any other hospitals. With just a few isolated exceptions, all of the other hospitals on Earth don't publish patient outcome statistics in the first place.

VISITOR: ... But... then—*what are they even selling?*

SIMPLICIO: Hold on. If you reward the doctors with the highest patient survival rates, won't they just reject all the patients with poor prognoses?

VISITOR: Obviously you don't evaluate raw survival rates. You have Diagnosticians who estimate prognosis categories and are rated on their predictive accuracy, and Treatment Planners and Surgeons who are rated on their *relative* outcomes, and you have the outcomes evaluated by a third party, and—

CECIE: In our world, there's no separation of powers where one person assigns patients a prognosis category and has their prediction record tracked, and another person does their best to treat them and has their treatment record tracked. So hospitals don't publish any performance statistics, and patients choose the hospital closest to their house that takes their workplace's insurance, and nobody has any financial incentive to decrease the number of patient deaths from sloppy surgeons or central line infections. When anesthesiologists in particular did happen to start tracking patient outcomes, they adopted some simple monitoring standards and subsequently decreased their fatality rates by a factor of *one hundred*.[28] But that's just anesthesiologists, not, say, cardiac surgeons.

With cardiac surgeons, a group of researchers recently figured out how to detect when the most senior cardiac surgeons were at conferences, and found that the death rates went down while the most senior cardiac surgeons

---

[28] From Hyman and Silver, "You Get What You Pay For" (http://scholarlycommons.law. wlu.edu/cgi/viewcontent.cgi?article=1469&context=wlulr):

> By the 1950s, death rates ranged between 1 and 10 per 10,000 encounters. Anesthesia mortality stabilized at this rate for more than two decades.
>
> Mortality and morbidity rates fell again after a 1978 article reframed the issue of anesthesia safety as one of human factor analysis. In the mid-1980s, the American Society of Anesthesiologists (ASA) promulgated standards of optimal anesthesia practice that relied heavily on systems-based approaches for preventing errors. Because patients frequently sued anesthetists when bad outcomes occurred and because deviations from the ASA guidelines made the imposition of liability much more likely, anesthetists had substantial incentives to comply.
>
> [… W]e should consider why anesthesia mortality stabilized at a rate more than one hundred times higher than its current level for more than two decades. The problem was not lack of information. To the contrary, anesthesia safety was studied extensively during the period. A better hypothesis is that anesthetists grew accustomed to a mortality rate that was exemplary by health care standards, but that was still higher than it should have been. From a psychological perspective, this low frequency encouraged anesthetists to treat each bad outcome as a tragic but unforeseen and unpreventable event. Indeed, anesthetists likely viewed each individual bad outcome as the manifestation of an irreducible baseline rate of medical mishap.

Hyman and Silver note other possible factors behind the large change, e.g., the fact that the person responsible for mishaps was often easy to identify since there tended to be only one anesthetist per procedure, and that "because surgical patients had no on-going relationships with their anesthetist, victims were particularly likely to sue."

were away.[29] But our scientists have to use special tricks if they want to find out any facts like that.

VISITOR: Do your *patients* not care if they live or die?

CECIE: Robin Hanson has a further thesis about how what people really want from medicine is reassurance rather than statistics. But I'm not sure that hypothesis is necessary to explain this particular aspect of the problem. If no hospital offers statistics, then you have no baseline to compare to if one hospital *does* start offering statistics. You'd just be looking at an alarming-looking percentage for how many patients die, with no idea of whether that's a better percentage or a worse percentage. Terrible marketing! Especially compared to that other hospital across town that just smiles at you reassuringly.

No hospital would benefit from being the *first* to publish statistics, so none of them do.

VISITOR: Your world has literally zero market demand for empirical evidence?

CECIE: Not zero, no. But since publishing scary numbers would be bad marketing for *most* patients, and hospitals are heavily regional, they all go by the majority preference to not hear about the statistics.

VISITOR: I confess I'm having some trouble grasping the concept of a market consisting of opaque boxes allegedly containing goods, in which nobody publishes what is inside the boxes.

CECIE: Hospitals don't publish prices either, in most cases.

VISITOR: …

CECIE: Yeah, it's pretty bad even by Earth standards.

VISITOR: You literally don't *have* a healthcare market. Nobody knows what outcomes are being sold. Nobody knows what the prices are.

---

[29] See Jena, Prasad, Goldman, and Romley, "Mortality and Treatment Patterns Among Patients Hospitalized With Acute Cardiovascular Conditions During Dates of National Cardiology Meetings" (http://jamanetwork.com/journals/jamainternalmedicine/fullarticle/2038879).

CECIE: I guess we could call that Total Market Failure? As in, things have gone so wrong that there's literally no supply-demand matching or price-equilibrating mechanism remaining, even though money is still changing hands.

And while I wish that this phenomenon of "you simply don't have a market" were only relevant to healthcare and not to other facets of our civilization... well, it's not.

vi. Absence of (meta-)competition

VISITOR: I suppose I can imagine imagine a hypothetical world in which *one* country screws things up as badly as you describe. But your planet has multiple governments, I thought. Or did I misunderstand that? Why wouldn't patients emigrate to—or just *visit*—countries that made better hospitals legal?

CECIE: The forces acting on governments with high technology levels are mostly the same between countries, so all the governments of those countries tend to have their medical system screwed up in mostly the same way (not least because they're imitating each other). Some aspects of dysfunctional insurance and payment policies are special to the US, but even the relatively functional National Health System in Britain still has failure of professional specialization. (Though they at least don't require doctors to have philosophy degrees.)

VISITOR: Is there not *one* government that would allow a reasonably designed hospital staffed by specialists instead of generalists?

CECIE: It wouldn't be enough to just have one government's okay. You'd need some way to initially train your workers, despite none of our world's medical schools being set up to train them. A majority of legislators won't benefit *personally* from deciding to let you try your new hospital in their country. Furthermore, you couldn't just go around raising money from rich countries for a venture in a poor country, because rich countries have elaborate regulations on who's allowed to raise money for business ventures through equity sales. The fundamental story is that everything, everywhere, is covered with varying degrees of molasses, and to do any novel thing you have to get around all of the molasses streams *simultaneously*.

VISITOR: So it's impossible to test a functional hospital design *anywhere on the planet?*

CECIE: But of course.

VISITOR: I must still be missing something. I just don't understand why all of the people with economics training on your planet can't go off by themselves and establish their own hospitals. Do you literally have people occupying every square mile of land?

CECIE: ... How do I phrase this...

All useful land is already claimed by some national government, in a way that the international order recognizes, whether or not that land is inhabited. No relevant decisionmaker has a personal incentive to allow there to be unclaimed land. Those countries will defend even a very small patch of that claimed land using all of the military force their country has available, and the international order will see you as the aggressor in that case.

VISITOR: Can you *buy* land?

CECIE: You can't buy the sovereignty on the land. Even if you had a *lot* of money, any country poor enough and desperate enough to consider your offer might just steal your stuff after you moved in.

Negotiating the right to bring in weapons to defend yourself in this kind of scenario would be even more unthinkable, and would spark international outrage that could prevent you from trading with other countries.

To be clear, it's not that there's a global dictator who prevents new countries from popping up; but every potentially useful part of every land is under *some* system's control, and all of those systems would refuse you the chance to set up your own alternative system, for very similar reasons.

VISITOR: So there's no way for your planet to *try* different ways of doing things, *anywhere*. You literally cannot run experiments about things like this.

CECIE: Why would there be? Who would decide that, and how would they personally benefit?

VISITOR: That sounds *extremely* alarming. I mean, difficulties of adoption are one thing, but not even being able to *try* new things and see what happens... Shouldn't everyone on your planet be able to detect at a glance how horrible things have become? Can this type of disaster really stand up to *universal* agreement that something is wrong?

CECIE: I'm afraid that our civilization doesn't have a sufficiently stirring and narratively satisfying conception of the valor of "testing things" that our people would be massively alarmed by its impossibility. And now, Visitor, I hope we've bottomed out the general concept of why people can't do things differently—the local system's equilibrium is broken, *and* the larger system's equilibrium makes it impossible to flee the game.

VISITOR: Okay, look... despite everything you've said so far, I still have some trouble understanding why doctors and parents can't just *not* kill the babies. I manage to get up every single morning and successfully not kill any babies. It's not as hard as it sounds.

CECIE: I worry you're starting to think like Simplicio. You can't just *not* kill babies and expect to get away with it.

SIMPLICIO: I actually agree with Cecie here. The evil people behind the system hate those who defy them by behaving differently; there's no way they'd countenance anyone departing from the norm. What we really need is a revolution, so we can depose our corrupt overlords, and finally be free to coordinate, and...!

CECIE: There's no need to add in any evil conspiracy hypotheses here. It's sufficient to note that the system is *in equilibrium* and it has *causes* for the equilibrium settling there—causes, if not justifications. You can't go against the system's default without going against the forces that underpin that default. A doctor who gives a baby a nutrition formula that isn't FDA-approved will lose their job. A hospital that doesn't fire that kind of doctor will be sued. A scientist that writes proposals for a big, expensive, definitive study won't get a grant, and while they were busy writing those failed grant proposals, they'll have lost their momentum toward tenure. So no, you can't just try out a competing policy of not killing babies. Not more than once.

VISITOR: *Have* you tried?

CECIE: No.

VISITOR: But—

CECIE: Anyway, from my perspective, it's no surprise if you don't yet feel like you understand. We've only *begun* to survey the malfunctions of the whole system, which would further include the FDA, and the clinical trials, and the *p*-hacking. And the way venture capital is structured, and equity-market regulations. And the insurance companies, and the tax code. And the corporations who contract with the insurance companies. And the corporations' employees. And the politicians. And the voters.

VISITOR: … Consider me impressed that your planet managed to reach this level of dysfunction without *actually physically bursting into flames.*

vii. Sticky traditions in belief-dependent Nash equilibria without common knowledge

CECIE: I could talk next about a tax system that makes it cheaper for corporations to pay for care instead of patients, and how that sets up a host of "decisionmaker is not the beneficiary" problems. But I suspect a lot of people reading this conversation understand that part already, so instead I'll turn my attention to venture capital.

VISITOR: It sounds like the "politicians" and the "voters" might be a more key issue, if the cultural translator is right about what those correspond to.

CECIE: Ah! But it turns out that venture capitalists and startups can be seen as a simpler version of voters and politicians, so it's better to consider entrepreneurs first.

Besides, at this point I imagine the Visitor is wondering, "Why can't anyone *make any money* by saving those babies? Doesn't your society have a profit incentive that fixes this?"

VISITOR: Actually, I don't think that *was* high on my list of questions. It's understood among my people that not every problem is one you can make a profit by fixing—*persistent* societal problems tend to be ones that don't have easily capturable profits corresponding to their solution.

I mean, *yes*, if this was all happening on our world and it wasn't already being addressed by the Serious People, then somebody *would* just mix the bleeping nutrients and sell it to the bleeping parents for bleeping money. But at this point I've already guessed that's going to be illegal, or saving babies using money is going to be associated with the wrong Tower and therefore unprestigious, or your parents are using a particular kind of statistical analysis that requires baby sacrifices, or whatever.

CECIE: Hey, details matter!

VISITOR: (*in sad reflection*) Do they? Do they really? Isn't there some point where you just admit you can't stop killing babies and it doesn't really matter why?

CECIE: No. You can *never* say that if you want to go on being a cynical economist.

Now, there are several different kinds of molasses covering the world of startups and venture capital. It's the *tradition-bound* aspects of that ecosystem that we'll find especially interesting, since according to its own ideology, venture capitalists are supposed to chase strange new ideas that other venture capitalists don't believe in. Walking through the simpler case of venture capital will help us understand the more complex reasons why voters and politicians are nailed into their own equilibria, underpinning the ultimate reasons why nobody can change the laws that prevent change.

VISITOR: (*gazing off into the distance*) ... I wonder if maybe there are some worlds that can't be saved.

CECIE: Suppose it's widely believed that the most successful entrepreneurs have red hair. If you're an unusually smart venture capital company that realizes that, *a priori*, hair color doesn't seem like it should correlate to entrepreneurial ability, you might think you could make an excess profit by finding some overlooked entrepreneur with blonde hair.

The key insight here is that venture capital is a *multi-stage* process. There's the initial or pre-seed round, the seed round, the Series A, the Series B, the middle rounds, the Series C... and if the startup fails to raise money on any of those rounds before they become durably profitable, they're dead. What this means is that the seed-round investors need to consider the probability that the company can successfully raise a Series A. If the angels invest in the seed round of a company whose entrepreneurs don't have red hair, that company won't be able to raise a Series A and will go bust and the angel investment will be worthless. So the angel investors need to decide where to invest, and what price to offer, based partially on their beliefs about what most Series A investors believe.

SIMPLICIO: Ah, I've heard of this. It's called a Keynesian beauty contest, where everyone tries to pick the contestant they expect everyone else to pick. A parable illustrating the massive, pointless circularity of the paper game called the stock market, where there's no objective except to buy the pieces of paper you'll think other people will want to buy.

CECIE: No, there are real returns on stocks—usually in the forms of buybacks and acquisitions, nowadays, since dividends are tax-disadvantaged. If the stock market has the nature of a self-fulfilling prophecy, it's only to the extent that high stock prices directly benefit companies, by letting the company get more capital or issue bonds at lower interest. If not for the direct effect that stock prices had on company welfare, it wouldn't matter at all to a 10-year investor what other investors believe today. If stock prices had zero effect on company welfare, you'd be happy to buy the stock that nobody else believed in, and wait for that company to have real revenues and retained assets that everyone else could see 10 years later.

SIMPLICIO: But *nobody* invests on a 10-year horizon! Even pension companies invest to manage the pension manager's bonus this year!

VISITOR: Surely the recursive argument is obvious? If most managers invest with 1-year lookahead, a smarter manager can make a profit in 1 year by investing with a 2-year lookahead, and can continue to extract value until there's no predictable change from 2-year prices to 1-year prices.

CECIE: In the entrepreneurial world, startups are killed outright, very quickly, by the equivalent of low stock prices. *And* for legal reasons there are no hedge funds that can adjust market prices en masse, so the recursive argument doesn't apply. The upshot is that seed investors have a *strong* incentive to care about what Series A investors think. If the entrepreneurs don't fit the stereotype of cool entrepreneurs who have red hair, you can't make an excess return by going against the popular misapprehension, because the startup will die in the next funding round.

The key phenomenon underlying the social molasses is that there's a self-reinforcing equilibrium of beliefs. Maybe a *lot* of the Series A investors think the idea of entrepreneurs needing to have red hair is objectively silly. But they expect Series B investors to believe it. So the Series A investors don't invest in blonde-haired entrepreneurs. So the seed investors are right to believe that "Series A investors won't invest in blonde-haired companies" even if a lot of the reason why Series A investors aren't investing is not that they believe the stereotype but that they believe that Series B investors believe the stereotype. And from the outside, of course, all that investors can *see* is that most investors aren't investing in blonde-haired entrepreneurs—which just goes to reinforce everyone's belief that everyone else believes that red-haired entrepreneurs do better.[30]

---

[30] See Glenn Loury's *The Anatomy of Racial Inequality* for an early discussion of this issue. Note that some venture capitalists I've spoken to endorse this as an account of VC dysfunction, while others have different hypotheses.

VISITOR: And you can't just have everyone say those exact words aloud, in unison, and simultaneously wake up from the dream?

SIMPLICIO: I'm afraid people don't understand recursion as well as that would require.

CECIE: Perhaps, Simplicio, it is only that most VCs believe that most other VCs don't understand recursion; that would have much the same effect in practice.

SIMPLICIO: Or maybe most people *are* too stupid to understand recursion. Is that something you'd be able to accept, if it were true?

CECIE: Regardless, on a larger scale, what we're seeing is an extra stickiness that results when the incentive to try an innovation requires you to believe that *other people will believe* the innovation will work. An equilibrium like that can be *much stickier* than a scenario where, if *you* believe that a project will succeed, *you* have an incentive to try it *even if* other people expect the project to fail.

Stereotypically, the startup world is supposed to consist of heroes producing an excess return by pursuing ideas that nobody else believes in. In reality, the multi-stage nature of venture capital makes it very easy for the field to end up pinned to traditions about whether entrepreneurs ought to have red hair—not because everyone believes it, but because everyone believes that everyone believes it.

viii. First-past-the-post and wasted votes

VISITOR: Does this feed back into our primary question of why your society can't stop itself from feeding poisonous substances to babies?

CECIE: It's true that venture capitalists are now collectively skeptical of attempts at new drug development, but the real problem (at least for cases like this) is the enormous cost of approval and the long delays the FDA causes.[31] The actual reason I went into this is that by understanding venture capitalists and entrepreneurs, we can understand the more complex case of voters and politicians. Which is the key to the *political* equilibrium that pins down the FDA, and all the other laws that prevent anyone from doing better. Not always, but quite often, the ultimate foundations of failure trace back to the molasses covering voters and politicians.

SIMPLICIO: I'd like to offer, throughout whatever theory follows, the alternative hypothesis that voters are *in fact* just fools, sheep, and knaves. I mean, you should at least be considering that possibility.

CECIE: The simplest way of understanding the analogy between venture capitalists and voters is that voters have to vote for politicians that are electable.

VISITOR: Uh, what? When you write down your preference ordering on elected representatives, you need to put politicians that other voters prefer at the top of your preference ordering?

CECIE: Yes, that's pretty much what it amounts to. In the US, at least, elections are run on what's known as a "first-past-the-post" voting system. Whoever gets the most votes in the contest wins. People who study voting systems widely agree that first-past-the-post is among the *worst* voting systems—it's provably impossible for one voting system to have all the intuitively good properties at once, but FPTP is one of the *most* broken.

VISITOR: Why not vote to change the voting system, then?

---

[31] Carl Shulman argues that the FDA's clinical trial requirements probably *aren't* the reason for recent decades' slowdown in the development of cool new drugs, given that increased regulation seems to have coincided with but not substantially accelerated the declining efficiency of pharmaceutical research and development (https://www.nature.com/nrd/journal/v11/n3/fig_tab/nrd3681_F1.html). Shulman suggests that Baumol's cost disease and diminishing returns play a larger role in the R&D slowdown.

The FDA's clinical trial requirements are much more likely to play a central role in limiting access to non-patented substances, though it's worth noting here that the FDA has gotten faster than it used to be (https://www.forbes.com/sites/matthewherper/2012/06/19/more-proof-fda-is-faster-than-other-regulators/).

CECIE: I'll get to that!

There are several ways of explaining what's wrong with FPTP, but a lovely explanation I recently encountered phrases the explanation in terms of "wasted votes"—the total number of votes that can be removed without changing the outcome.

The two classic forms of gerrymandering are *cracking* and *packing*. Let's say the parties are Green and Orange, and the Green party is in charge of drawing the voting boundaries. As a Green, you want to draw up districts such that Green politicians win with 55% of the vote—with some room for error, but not all that much—and for Orange politicians to win with 100% of the vote.

SIMPLICIO: Ah, so that the Orange politicians won't need to be responsive to Orange voters because their re-election is nearly guaranteed, right?

CECIE: No, the plot is far more diabolical than that. Consider a district of 100,000 people, where a Green politician wins with 55% of the vote. When 50,001 Green voters had cast their ballots, the election was already decided, under first-past-the-post, so the next 4,999 Green votes are "wasted"—this is to be understood as a technical term, not a moral judgment—in that they don't further change the outcome. Then 45,000 Orange votes are also "wasted," in that they don't change the outcome. And also, one notes, those Orange voters don't get the representative they wanted.

In an Orange district of 100,000 where the politician wins with 100% of the vote, there are 50,000 potent Orange votes and 50,000 wasted Orange votes. In total, there are 50,000 potent Green votes, 5,000 wasted Green votes, 50,000 potent Orange votes, and 95,000 wasted Orange votes. On a larger scale, this means that you can control a majority of a state legislature with slightly more than 1/4 of the votes—just have 55% of the districts containing 55% Green voters, with everything else solid Orange.

VISITOR: And then this quarter of the population rules cruelly over the remaining three-quarters, who in turn lack the weapons to rise up?

CECIE: No, the real damage is far subtler. Let's say that Alice, Bob, and Carol have taken time off from their cryptographic shenanigans to run for political office. Alice is in the lead, followed by Bob and then by Carol. Suppose Dennis prefers Carol to Bob, and Bob to Alice. But Dennis can't actually write "Carol > Bob > Alice" on a slip of paper that gets processed by a trivially more sophisticated voting system. Dennis is only allowed to write down one candidate's name, and that's his vote. Under a system where the candidate with the most votes wins, and there's uncertainty about which of the two frontrunners might win, *all votes for whoever is in third place will be wasted votes*, and this fact is predictable to the voters.

VISITOR: Ah, I see. That's why you introduced your peculiar multi-stage system of venture capital, which I assume must be held in place by laws forbidding anyone else to go off and organize their own financial system differently, and observed how it creates a sticky equilibrium in which financiers must believe that other financiers will believe in a startup.

If Dennis doesn't believe that other "voters" will believe in Carol, Dennis will vote for Bob, which makes your politics stickier than a system in which "voters" were permitted to support the people they actually liked.

CECIE: Well, you see the analogy, but I'm not sure you appreciate the true depth of the horror.

VISITOR: I'm sure I don't.

CECIE: The upshot of first-past-the-post is typically a political system dominated by exactly two parties.

VISITOR: Parties?

SIMPLICIO: Entities that tell sheep who to vote for.

CECIE: In elections that have a single winner, votes for any candidate who isn't one of the top two choices are wasted. In a representative democracy where districts vote on representatives who vote on laws, the dynamics of the district vote are then influenced by the dynamics of the national vote. Even if a third-party candidate could win a district, they wouldn't have anyone to work with in the legislature, and so their votes would generally be wasted.

In the absence of a way to solve a large coordination problem, there's no way for a third party to gain marginal influence over time. Each individual who considers voting for a third-party candidate knows they'll be wasting their vote. This also means that third parties can't field good candidates, since potential candidates know they'd be running to lose, which is stressful and unrewarding for people with better life options. And that's a sufficient multi-factor system to prevent strong third parties from arising. When you're not allowed to vote for Carol, who you actually like, you'll vote for whichever of Alice and Bob you dislike the least.

The resulting equilibrium... well, Abramowitz and Webster found that what mainly predicted voting behavior wasn't how much the voter liked their preferred party, but how much they disliked the opposing party.[32] Essentially, the US has two major voting factions, "people who hate Red politicians" and "people who hate Blue politicians." When the Red politicians do something that Red-haters *really* dislike, that gives the Blue politicians more leeway to do additional things that Red-haters mildly dislike, which can give the Red politicians more leeway of their own, and so the whole thing slides sideways.

SIMPLICIO: Looking at the abstract of that Abramowitz and Webster paper, isn't one of their major findings that this type of hate-based polarization has *increased* a great deal over the last twenty years?

CECIE: Well, yes. I don't claim to know exactly why that happened, but I suspect the Internet had something to do with it.

In the US, the current two parties froze into place in the early twentieth century—before then, there was sometimes turnover (or threatened turnover). I suspect that the spread of radio broadcasting had something to do with the freeze. If you imagine a country in the pre-telegraph days, then it might be possible for third-party candidates to take hold in one state, then in nearby

---

[32] Abramowitz and Webster, "All Politics is National" (http://stevenwwebster.com/research/all_politics_is_national.pdf).

states, and so a global change starts from a local nucleus. A national radio system makes politics less local.

The Internet might have pushed this phenomenon further and caused most of politics to be about the same national issues, which in turn reinforces the Red-vs.-Blue dynamic that allows each party to sustain itself on hatred for the other.

But that's just me trying to eyeball the phenomenon using American history—I haven't studied it. Other countries that also have the radio and Internet and similar electoral dynamics do manage to have more than two relevant parties, possibly because of dynamics that cause the votes of third-party politicians to be less wasted.

SIMPLICIO: Isn't the solution here obvious, though? All of these problems are caused by voters' willingness to compromise on their principles and accept the lesser of two evils.

CECIE: Would things be better if people chose the greater of two evils? If they acted ineffectually against that greater evil? The Nash equilibrium isn't an illusion. Individuals would do worse by playing away from that Nash equilibrium. Wasted votes *are* wasted. The current system *is* an effective trap and the voters *are* trapped. They can't just wish their way out of that trap.

There doesn't need to be any way for good to win; and if there isn't, the lesser evil really is the best that voters can do. Pretending otherwise may feel righteous, but it doesn't change the equilibrium.

VISITOR: Just one second. Isn't this all window dressing, compared to the issue of whatever true ruler imposes these rules on the "voters"? Like, if you put me into an elaborate cage that gives me an electric shock each time I vote for Carol, obviously the person who really controls the system is whoever put the cage in place and determines which politicians you can vote for without electric shocks.

SIMPLICIO: I like the way you think.

CECIE: It's not *quite* true to say that the system is self-reinforcing and that the voters are the sole instrument of their own destruction. But the lack of any obvious, individual tyrant who personally decides who you're allowed to vote for has indeed caused many voters to believe that they are in control. I mean, they don't *feel* like they're in control, but they think that "the voters" select politicians.

They aren't able to personalize a complicated bad equilibrium as a tyrant—not like they would blame a jeweled king who was standing in the polling booth, ready to give them an electric shock if they wrote down Carol's name.

Inspired by Allan Ginsberg's poem *Moloch*, Scott Alexander once wrote of coordination failures:

> Moloch is introduced as the answer to a question—C. S. Lewis' question in Hierarchy Of Philosophers—*what does it?* Earth could be fair, and all men glad and wise. Instead we have prisons, smokestacks, asylums. What sphinx of cement and aluminum breaks open their skulls and eats up their imagination?
>
> And Ginsberg answers: *Moloch does it.*
>
> There's a passage in the *Principia Discordia* where Malaclypse complains to the Goddess about the evils of human society. "Everyone is hurting each other, the planet is rampant with injustices, whole societies plunder groups of their own people, mothers imprison sons, children perish while brothers war."
>
> The Goddess answers: "What is the matter with that, if it's what you want to do?"
>
> Malaclypse: "But nobody wants it! Everybody hates it!"
>
> Goddess: "Oh. Well, then stop."
>
> The implicit question is—if everyone hates the current system, who perpetuates it? And Ginsberg answers: "Moloch." It's powerful not because it's correct—nobody literally thinks an ancient Carthaginian demon causes everything—but because thinking of

the system as an agent throws into relief the degree to which the system *isn't* an agent.[33]

Scott Alexander saw the face of the Enemy, and he gave it a name—thinking that perhaps that would help.

VISITOR: So if you did do this to yourselves, all by yourselves with no external empire to prevent you from doing anything differently by force of arms, then *why can't you just vote to change the voting rules?* No, never mind "voting"—why can't you all just *get together and change everything, period?*

CECIE: It's true that concepts like these are nontrivial to understand.

It's not obvious to me that people *couldn't possibly* understand them, if somebody worked for a while on creating diagrams and videos.

But the bigger problem is that people wouldn't know they could trust the diagrams and videos. I suspect some of the dynamics in entrepreneur-land are there because many venture capitalists run into entrepreneurs that are smarter than them, but who still have bad startups. A venture capitalist who believes clever-sounding arguments will soon be talked into wasting a lot of money. So venture capitalists learn to distrust clever-sounding arguments because they can't distinguish lies from truth, when they're up against entrepreneurs who are smarter than them.

Similarly, the average politician is smarter than the average voter, so by now most voters are just accustomed to a haze of plausible-sounding arguments. It's not that you can't possibly explain a Nash equilibrium. It's that there are too many people advocating changes in the system for their own reasons, who could also draw diagrams that sounded equally convincing to someone who didn't already understand Nash equilibria. Any talk of systemic change on this level would just be lost in a haze of equally plausible-sounding-to-the-average-voter blogs, talking about how quantitative easing will cause hyperinflation.

---

[33] See Scott Alexander's "Meditations on Moloch" (https://slatestar-codex.com/2014/07/30/meditations-on-moloch/).

VISITOR: Maybe it's naive of me... but I can't help but think... that *surely* there must be *some* breaking point in this system you describe, of voting for the less bad of two awful people, where the candidates just get worse and worse over time. At some point, shouldn't this be trumped by the "voters" just getting completely fed up? A spontaneous equilibrium-breaking, where they just didn't vote for either of the standard lizards no matter what?

CECIE: Perhaps so! But my own cynicism can't help but suspect that this "trumping" phenomenon of which you speak would be even worse.

SIMPLICIO: I have a technical objection to your ascribing all these sins to first-past-the-post voting rather than, say, the personal vices of the voters. There are numerous parliamentary democracies outside the United States that practice proportional representation, where a party getting 30% of the votes gets 30% of the seats in parliament. And *they* don't seem to have solved these problems.

CECIE: Omegaven does happen to be approved in Europe, however. Like, they are not in fact killing those particular babies—

SIMPLICIO: Oh, *come on!* Yes, the European equivalent of the US's FDA happens to be a bit less stupid. Lots of other things in European countries happen to be more stupid. Indeed, I'd say that in Europe you have much *crazier* people getting seats in parliaments, compared to the United States. The problem isn't the voting system. The problem is the *voters*.

CECIE: There are indeed some voters who want stupid things, and under the European system, their voice can be heard. There are also voters who want smart things and whose voices can be heard, like in the Pirate Party in Finland. But European parliamentary systems have *different* problems stemming from *different* systemic flaws.

Proportional representation would be a good system for a legislature that needed to repeatedly vote on laws, where different legislators could form different coalitions for each vote. If instead you demand that a majority coalition "form a government" to appoint an executive, then you need to give concessions to some factions, while other factions get frozen out. I'm not necessarily saying that it would be *easy* to fix all the problems simultaneously. Still, I imagine that a proportionally represented legislature, *combined* with an executive elected at-large by Condorcet voting, might possibly be less stupid—

SIMPLICIO: Or maybe it would just give stupid voters a louder voice. I don't like the evil conspiracy of the press and political elites that governs my country from the shadows, but I *am* willing to consider the proposition that the alternative is Donald Trump. I mean, I intend to go on fighting the Conspiracy about many specific issues. But if you're proposing a reform that puts more power into the hands of sheep not yet awakened, the results could be even worse.

CECIE: Well, I agree that the design of well-functioning political systems is hard. Singapore might be the best-governed country in the world, and their history is approximately, "Lee Kuan Yew gained very strong individual power over a small country, and unlike the hundreds of times in the history of Earth when that went horribly wrong, Lee Kuan Yew happened to know some economics." But the Visitor asked me why we were killing babies, and I tried to answer in terms of the system that obtained in the part of the world that was actually killing those babies. *You* asked why Europe wasn't a paradise since it used proportional representation, and my answer is that parliamentary systems have their own design flaws that induce a different kind of dysfunction.

SIMPLICIO: Then if both systems are bad, how does your hypothesis have any observable consequences?

CECIE: Because different systems are bad in different ways. When you have a "crazy" new idea, whether it's good or bad, the European parliaments will be allowed to talk about it first. Whether that's Omegaven, basic income, gay marriage, legalized prostitution, ending the war on drugs, land value taxes, or fascist nationalism, you are more likely to find it talked about in systems of proportional representation. It also happens to be true that those governments bloat up faster because of the repeated bribes required to hold the "governing coalition" together, but that's a *different* problem.

ix. The Overton window

SIMPLICIO: I'm beginning to experience the same sort of confusion as the Visitor about your view of the world, Conventional Cynical Economist. If voters weren't stupid, the world would look very different than it does.

If the ultimate source of stupidity were poorly designed governmental structures, then average voters would sound smarter than average politicians. I don't think that's *actually* true.

CECIE: There are deeper forms of psychological molasses that generalize beyond first-past-the-post political candidates. The still greater force locking bad political systems into place is an equilibrium of silence about policies that aren't "serious."

A journalist thinks that a candidate who talks about ending the War on Drugs isn't a "serious candidate." And the newspaper won't cover that candidate because the newspaper itself wants to look serious... or they think voters won't be interested because everyone knows that candidate can't win, or something? Maybe in a US-style system, only contrarians and other people who lack the social skill of getting along with the System are voting for Carol, so Carol is uncool the same way Velcro is uncool and so are all her policies and ideas? I'm not sure exactly what the journalists are thinking subjectively, since I'm not a journalist. But if an existing politician talks about a policy outside of what journalists think is appealing to voters, the journalists think the politician has committed a gaffe, and they write about this sports blunder by the politician, and the actual voters take their cues from that. So no politician talks about things that a journalist believes it would be a blunder for a politician to talk about. The space of what it isn't a "blunder" for a politician to talk about is conventionally termed the "Overton window."

SIMPLICIO: It's all well and good to talk about complicated clever things, Cynical Economist, but what explanatory power does all this added complexity have? Why postulate politicians who believe that journalists believe that voters won't take something seriously? Why not just say that people are sheep?

CECIE: To name a recent example from the United States, it explains how, one year, gay marriage is this taboo topic, and then all of a sudden there's a huge upswing in everyone being *allowed* to talk about it for the first time and shortly afterwards it's a done deal. If you suppose that a huge number of people really did hate gay marriage deep down, or that all the politicians mouthing off about the sanctity of marriage were engaged in a dark conspiracy, then why the sudden change?

With my more complicated model, we can say, "An increasing number of people over time thought that gay marriage was pretty much okay. But while that group didn't have a majority, journalists modeled a gay marriage endorsement as a 'gaffe' or 'unelectable', something they'd write about in the sports-coverage overtone of a blunder by the other team—"

SIMPLICIO: Ah, so you say it was a conspiracy by evil journalists?

CECIE: No! Those journalists weren't *consciously deciding* the equilibrium. The journalists were writing "serious" articles, i.e., articles about Alice and Bob rather than Carol. The equilibrium *consisted of* the journalists writing sports coverage of elections, where everything is viewed through the lens of a zero-sum competition for votes between Alice's team and Bob's team. Viewed through that lens, the journalists thought a gay marriage endorsement would be a blunder. And if you do something that enough journalists think is a political blunder, it *is* a political blunder. The journalists' sports coverage will describe you as an incompetent politician, and primates instinctively want to ally with likely winners. Which meant the equilibrium could have a sharp tipover point, *without* most of the actual population changing their minds sharply about gay marriage in that particular year. The support level went over a threshold where somebody tested the waters and got away with it, and journalists began to suspect it wasn't a political blunder to support gay marriage, which let more politicians speak and get away with it, and then the *change of belief about what was inside the Overton window* snowballed. I think that's what we saw.

SIMPLICIO: Forgive me for resorting to Occam's Razor, but is it not simpler just to say that people's beliefs changed slowly until it reached some level where the military-industrial complex realized they couldn't win the battle to suppress gay marriage outright, and so stopped fighting?

CECIE: In a sense, that's not far off from what happened, except without the evil conspiracy part. We might or might not be approaching a similar tipover point about ending the War on Drugs—a long, slow, secular shift in opinion, followed by a sudden tipover point where journalists model politicians as being allowed to talk about it, which means that politicians *can* talk about it, and then a few years later everyone is acting like they always thought that way. At least, I *hope* that's where the current trend is leading.

SIMPLICIO: Several states have already passed laws legalizing marijuana. Why hasn't that already broken the Overton window?

CECIE: Because voter initiatives don't break the common belief about what it would be a "gaffe" for a *serious, national-level* politician to do.

ELIEZER: (*aside*) What broke the silence about artificial general intelligence (AGI) in 2014 wasn't Stephen Hawking writing a careful, well-considered essay about how this was a real issue. The silence only broke when Elon Musk tweeted about Nick Bostrom's *Superintelligence*, and then made an off-the-cuff remark about how AGI was "summoning the demon."

Why did that heave a rock through the Overton window, when Stephen Hawking couldn't? Because Stephen Hawking *sounded like* he was trying hard to appear sober and serious, which signals that this is a subject you have to be careful not to gaffe about. And then Elon Musk was like, "*Whoa, look at that apocalypse over there!!*" After which there was the equivalent of journalists trying to pile on, shouting, "A gaffe! A gaffe! A... gaffe?" and finding out that, in light of recent news stories about AI and in light of Elon Musk's good reputation, people weren't backing them up on that gaffe thing.

Similarly, to heave a rock through the Overton window on the War on Drugs, what you need is not state propositions (although those do help) or articles in *The Economist*. What you need is for some "serious" politician to say, "This is dumb," and for the journalists to pile on shouting, "A gaffe! A gaffe... a gaffe?" But it's a grave personal risk for a politician to test whether the public atmosphere has changed enough, and even if it worked, they'd capture very little of the human benefit for themselves.

VISITOR: So... if this is the key meta-level problem... then why can't your civilization just *consider and solve this entire problem on the meta level?*

CECIE: Oh, I'm afraid that this entire meta-problem isn't the sort of thing the "leading candidates" Alice and Bob talk about, so the problem itself isn't viewed as serious. That is, journalists won't think it's serious. Meta-problems in general—even problems as simple as first-past-the-post versus instant runoff for particular electoral districts—are issues outside the Overton window. So the leading candidates Alice and Bob won't talk about organizational design reform, because it would be very damaging to their careers if they visibly focused their attention on issues that journalists don't think of as "serious."

VISITOR: Then perhaps the deeper question is, "Why does anyone listen to these 'journalists'?" You keep attributing power to them, but you haven't yet explained why they have that power under your equilibrium.

CECIE: People believe that other people believe what's in the newspapers. Well, no, that's too optimistic. A lot of people *do* believe what's in the newspapers, so long as it isn't about a topic regarding which they have any personal knowledge or expertise. The Gell-Mann Amnesia Effect is the term for how we read the paper about subjects we know about, and it's talking about how wet streets cause rain; and then we turn to the story about international affairs or dieting, and for some reason assume it's more accurate.

There's some level on which most people prefer to talk and believe within the same mental world as other people. Nowadays a lot of people believe what they read on, say, Tumblr, and hardly look at *The New York Times* at all. But even then they still believe that *other people* believe what's in *The New York Times*. That's what gives *The New York Times* its special power over the collective consciousness, far out of proportion to their dwindling readership or the vanishing real trust that individuals from various walks of life have in them—what's printed in *The New York Times* determines what people believe other people believe.

SIMPLICIO: Do you *truly* lay all the sins of humanity at the feet of all this weird recursion? Or is this just a sufficiently weird hypothesis that you find it more fun to think about than the alternatives?

CECIE: I'm not sure I'm pointing in exactly the right direction, but I feel that I'm pointing in the general direction of something that's truly important to the Visitor's most basic question. The Visitor keeps asking why, in some sense, on some sufficiently general level, we can't *just snap out of it*. And to put it in the sort of terms you yourself might want to use, Simplicio, if we're looking for an explanation of why we can't *just snap out of it*, then it might make sense to point to a bad Nash equilibrium covering our collective consciousness and discussion. I suspect that the recursion, the dependency on what people believe other people believe, has a lot to do with making that a *sticky* equilibrium a la venture capital.

ELIEZER: (*aside*) Returning to my day job: As of 2017, I pretty commonly hear from AI researchers who are worried about AGI safety, but who say that they don't dare say anything like that aloud. You could see this as either a good sign or a very bad sign, depending on how pessimistic or optimistic you previously were about the adequacy of academic discussion.

SIMPLICIO: But then what, on your view, is the better way?

CECIE: Again, I could pontificate about various ideas, but that's a *different and harder question* than looking at the actual equilibrium that currently obtains and forces doctors to poison babies. There doesn't have to be a better way.

x. Lower-hanging altruistic fruit and bigger problems

(The Visitor takes a deep breath. When the Visitor speaks again, it is louder.)

VISITOR: Then what about your *<untranslatable 17>*?

CECIE: Sorry? That word didn't come through.

VISITOR: What about everyone on your *entire planet* who could possibly care about babies dying?

So your medical specialists are borked. From the magic-tower analogy, I assume your systems of learning are borked, and that means most of the parents whose responsibility it is to protect the child are borked. Your politicians are borked. Your voters are borked. Your planet has no Serious People who could be trusted to try alternative shoe designs, let alone lead the way on any more complex coordination problem. Your prediction markets, I suppose, are somehow borked in a way that prevents anyone from making a profit by correcting inaccurate policy forecasts... maybe they forecast wrongly bad consequences to unpopular policies, which therefore never get implemented in a way that shows up the inaccurate prediction, since you don't have any way to test things on a smaller scale? Your economists must somehow be borked—

CECIE: It's more that nobody ever listens to us. They *pay us* and then they don't *listen to us*.

VISITOR: —and your financial system is borked so that nobody can make a profit on saving those babies or doing anything else useful. I'm not stupid. I've picked up on the pattern at this point.

But what about *everyone else?* There are seven *billion* people on your planet. How is it that *none* of them step up to save these babies from death and brain damage? How is your *entire planet* failing to solve this problem?

CECIE: That... sounds like a weird question, to an Earth person.

VISITOR: Whatever your problems are, surely out of seven billion human beings there have to be *some* who could *see* the problems as you've laid them out, who could try to rally others to the cause of saving those babies, who could do *whatever it took* to save them!

Even if your system declares that saving babies is only the responsibility of "doctors" or "politicians" or whoever is the Someone Else whose Problem it is, there's no law of physics that *stops* someone else from walking up to the problem and accepting responsibility for it. Out of seven billion people in your world, I can't believe that *literally all* of them are incapable of gathering together some friends and starting things down the path to getting a little fish oil into a baby's nutritional mixture!

ELIEZER: I think I'll step in myself at this point. There's one other very general conclusion we can draw from seeing this ever-growing heap of dead babies. We might say, "the inadequacy of the part implies the inadequacy of the whole"—as we've defined our terms, if a part of the system is inadequate in X lives saved for Y dollars, then the whole system is inadequate in X lives saved for Y dollars. Someone who is motivated and maximizing will first go after the biggest inadequacy *anywhere* that they think they can solve, and if they succeed, it pushes forward the adequacy frontier for the whole system. Thus, we can draw one other general conclusion from the observation that babies are still being fed soybean oil. We can conclude that everyone on the planet who is smart enough to understand this problem, and who cares about strangers' lives, and who maximizes over their opportunities, must have *something more important to do* than getting started on solving it.

VISITOR: (*aghast*) More important than saving hundreds of babies per year from dying or suffering permanent brain damage?

ELIEZER: The observation stands: there must be, in fact, literally nobody on Earth who can read Wikipedia entries and understand that omega-6 and omega-3 fats are different micronutrients, who also cares and maximizes and can head up new projects, who thinks that saving a few hundred babies per year from death and permanent brain damage is the most important thing they could do with their lives.

VISITOR: So you're implying...

ELIEZER: Well, mostly I'm implying that *maximizing* altruism is incredibly rare, especially when you also require sufficiently precise reasoning that you aren't limited to cases where the large-scale, convincing study has already been done; and then we're demanding the executive ability to start a new project on top of that. But yes, I'm also saying that here on Earth we have much more horrible problems to worry about.

CECIE: We've just been walking through a handful of lay economic concepts here, the kind whose structure I can explain in a few thousand words. If you truly perceived the world through the eyes of a conventional cynical economist, then the horrors, the abominations, the low-hanging fruits you saw unpicked would annihilate your very soul.

VISITOR: ...

ELIEZER: And then some of us have much, *much* more horrible problems to worry about. Problems that take *more* than reading Wikipedia entries to understand, so that the pool of potential solvers is even smaller. But even just considering this particular heap of dead babies, we know from observation that this part must be true: If you imagine everyone on Earth who fits the qualifications for the dead-baby problem—enough scientific literacy to understand relevant facts about metabolic pathways, *and* the caring, *and* the maximization, *and* enough scrappiness to be the first one who gets started on it, meeting in a conference room to divide up Earth's most important problems, with the first subgroup taking on the most neglected problems demanding the most specialized background knowledge, and the second taking on the second-most-incomprehensible set of problems, until the crowdedness of the previously most urgent problem decreases the marginal impact of further contributions to the point where the next-worst problem at that level of background knowledge and insight becomes attractive... and so on down the ladders of urgency inside the levels of discernment... then there must be such a long and terrible list of tasks left undone, and so few people to understand and care, that saving a few hundred babies per year from dying or suffering permanent brain damage didn't make the list. So it has been observed, and so it must be.

WANDERING BYSTANDER: (*interjecting*) But I just can't believe our planet would be that dysfunctional. Therefore, by backward chaining, I question the original observation on which you founded your inference. In particular, I'm starting to wonder whether omega-3 and omega-6 could *really* be such significantly different micronutrients. Maybe that's just a crackpot diet theory that somehow made it into Wikipedia, and actually all fats *are* pretty much the same, so there's nothing especially terrifying about the prospect of feeding babies exclusively fat from soybean oil instead of something more closely resembling the lipid profile of breast milk?

ELIEZER: Ah, yes. I'm glad you spoke up. I'll get to your modest proposal next.

4. Living in an Inadequate World

Be warned: Trying to put together a background model like the one I sketched in the previous chapter is a pretty perilous undertaking, especially if you don't have a professional economist checking your work at every stage.

Suppose I offered the following much simpler explanation of how babies are dying inside the US healthcare system:

What if parents don't really care about their babies?

Maybe parents don't bond to their babies so swiftly? Maybe they don't really care *that* much about those voiceless pink blobs in the early days? Maybe this is one of those things that people think they're *supposed* to feel very strongly, and yet the emotion isn't actually there. Maybe parents just sort of inwardly shrug when their infants die, and only pretend to be sad about it. If they really cared, wouldn't they demand a system that didn't kill babies?

In our taxonomy, this would be a "decisionmaker is not beneficiary" explanation, with the parents and doctors being the decisionmakers, and the babies being the beneficiaries.

A much simpler hypothesis, isn't it?

When we try to do inadequacy analysis, there is such a thing as *wrong guesses* and *false cynicism*.

I'm sure there are some parents who don't bond to their babies all that intensely. I'm sure some of them lie to themselves about that. But in the early days when Omegaven was just plain illegal to sell across state lines, some parents would drive for hours, every month, to buy Omegaven from the Boston Children's Hospital to take back to their home state. I, for one, would call that an *extraordinary effort*. Those parents went far outside their routine, beyond what the System would demand of them, beyond what the world was set up to support them doing by default. Most people won't make an effort that far outside their usual habits even if their own personal lives are at stake.

If parents are letting their babies die of liver damage *because the parents don't care*, we should find few extraordinary efforts in these and other cases of baby-saving. This is an observational consequence we can check, and the observational check fails to support the theory.

For a fixed amount of inadequacy, there is only so much dysfunction that needs to be invoked to explain it. By the nature of inadequacy there will usually be more than one thing going wrong at a time… but even so, there's only a bounded amount of failure to be explained. Every possible dysfunction is *competing* against every other possible dysfunction to explain the observed data. Sloppy cynicism will usually be wrong, just like your Facebook acquaintances who attribute civilizational dysfunctions to giant malevolent conspiracies.

If you're sloppy, then you're almost always going to find some way to conclude, "Oh, those physicists are just part of the broken academic system, what would they really know about the Higgs boson?" You will detect inadequacy every time you go looking for it, whether or not it's there. If you see the same vision wherever you look, that's the same as being blind.

i.

In most cases, you won't need to resort to complicated background analyses to figure out whether something is broken.

I mean, it's not like the only possible way one might notice that the US health care system is a vast, ill-conceived machine that is broken and also on fire is to understand microeconomics and predict *a priori* that aspects of this system design might promote inadequate equilibria. In real life, one notices the brokenness by reading economists who blog about the grinding gears and seas of flame, and listening to your friends sob about the screams coming from the ruins.

Then what good does it do to understand Moloch's toolbox? What's the point of the skill?

I suspect that for many people, the primary benefit of inadequacy analysis will be in undoing a mistake already made, where they disbelieve in inadequacy even when they're looking straight at it.

There are people who would simply never *try* to put up 130 light bulbs in their house—because if that worked, surely some good and diligent professional researcher would have already tried it. The medical system would have made it a standard treatment, right? The doctor would already know about it, right? And sure, sometimes people are stupid, but we're also people and we're also stupid so how could we amateurs possibly do better than current researchers on SAD, et cetera.

Often the most commonly applicable benefit from a fancy rational technique will be to cancel out fancy irrationality.[34] I expect that the most common benefit of inadequacy analysis will be to break a certain kind of blind trust—that is, trust arrived at by mental reasoning processes that are insensitive to whether you actually inhabit a universe that's worthy of that trust—and open people's eyes to the blatant brokenness of things that are easily *observed* to be broken. Understanding the background theory helps cancel out the elaborate arguments saying that you *can't* second-guess the European Central Bank even when it's straightforward to show how and why they're making a mistake.

Conversely, I've also watched some people plunge straight into problems that I'd guess were inexploitable, without doing the check, and then fail—usually falling prey to the Free Energy Fallacy, supposing that they can win just by doing better on the axis they care about. That subgroup might benefit, not from being told, "Shut up, you'll always fail, the answer is always no," but just from a reminder to *check* for signs of inexploitability.

---

[34] As an example, relatively few people in the world need well-developed skills at cognitive reductionism for the purpose of disassembling aspects of nature. The reason why *anyone else* needs to learn cognitive reductionism—the reason it's this big public epistemic hygiene issue—is that there are a lot of damaging supernatural beliefs that cognitive reductionism helps counter.

It may be that some of those people will end up always saying, "I can think of at least one Moloch's toolbox element in play, therefore this problem will be exploitable!" No humanly possible strictures of rationality can be strict enough to prevent a really determined person from shooting themselves in the foot. But it does help to be aware that the skill exists, before you start refining the skill.

Whether you're trying to move past modesty or overcome the Free Energy Fallacy:

- Step one is to realize that here is a place to build an explicit domain theory—to *want* to understand the meta-principles of free energy, the principles of Moloch's toolbox and the converse principles that imply real efficiency, and build up a model of how they apply to various parts of the world.

- Step two is to adjust your mind's exploitability detectors until they're not *always* answering, "You couldn't possibly exploit this domain, foolish mortal," or, "Why trust those hedge-fund managers to price stocks correctly when they have such poor incentives?"

And then you can move on to step three: the fine-tuning against reality.

ii.

In my past experience, I've both undershot and overshot the relative competence of doctors in the US medical system:

Anecdote 1: I once became very worried when my then-girlfriend got a headache and started seeing blobs of color, and when she drew the blobs they were left-right asymmetrical. I immediately started worrying about the asymmetry, thinking, "This is the kind of symptom I'd expect if someone had suffered damage to just one side of the brain." Nobody at the emergency room seemed very concerned, and she waited for a couple of hours to be seen, when I could remember reading that strokes had to be treated within the first few hours (better yet, minutes) to save as much brain tissue as possible.

What she was really experiencing, of course, was her first migraine. And I expect that every nurse we talked to *knew that*, but only a doctor is allowed to make *diagnoses*, so they couldn't legally *tell us*. I'd read all sorts of wonderful papers about exotic and illuminating forms of brain damage, but no papers about the *much more common* ailments that people in emergency rooms actually have. "Think horses, not zebras," as the doctors say.

Anecdote 2: I once saw a dermatologist for a dandruff problem. He diagnosed me with eczema, and gave me some steroid cream to put on my head for when the eczema became especially severe. It didn't cure the dandruff—but I'd seen a doctor, so I shrugged and concluded that there probably wasn't much to be done, since I'd already tried and failed using the big guns of the Medical System.

Eight years later, when I was trying to compound a ketogenic meal replacement fluid I'd formulated in an attempt to lose weight, my dandruff seemed to get worse. So I checked whether online paleo blogs had anything to say about treating dandruff via diet. I learned that a lot of dandruff is caused by the *Candida* fungus (which I'd never heard of), and that *the fungus eats ketones*. So if switching to a ketogenic diet (or drinking MCT oil, which gets turned into ketones) makes your dandruff worse, why, your dandruff is probably the *Candida* fungus. I looked up what kills *Candida*, found that I should use a shampoo containing ketoconazole, kept Googling, found a paper stating that 2% ketocanozole shampoo is an order of magnitude more effective than 1%, learned that only 1% ketocanozole shampoo was sold in the US, and ordered imported 2% Nizoral from Thailand via Amazon. Shortly thereafter, dandruff was no longer a significant issue for me and I could wear dark shirts without constantly checking my right shoulder for white specks. If my dermatologist knew anything about dandruff commonly being caused by a fungus, he never said a word.

From those two data points and others like them, I infer that medical competence—not medical absolute performance, but medical competence relative to what I can figure out by Googling—is high-variance. I shouldn't trust my doctor on significant questions without checking her diagnosis and treatment plan on the Internet, and I also shouldn't trust myself.

A lot of the times we put on our inadequacy-detecting goggles, we're deciding whether to trust some aspect of society to be more competent than ourselves. Part of the point of learning to think in economic terms about this question is to make it more natural to treat it as a technical question where specific lines of evidence can shift specific conclusions to varying degrees.

In particular, you don't need to be strictly better or worse than some part of society. The question isn't *about* ranking people, so you can be smarter in some ways and dumber in others. It can vary from minute to minute as the gods roll their dice.

By contrast, the modest viewpoint seems to me to have a very *social-status*-colored perspective on such things.

In the modest world, either you think you're better than doctors and all the civilization backing them, or you admit you're not as good and that you ought to defer to them.

If you don't defer to doctors, then you'll end up as one of those people who try feeding their children organic herbs to combat cancer; the outside view says that that's what happens to most non-doctors who dare to think they're *better* than doctors.

On the modest view, it's *not* that we hold up a thumb and eyeball the local competence level, based mostly on observation and a little on economic thinking; and then update on our observed relative performance; and sometimes say, "This varies a lot. I'll have to check each time."

Instead, every time you decide whether you think you can do better, *you are declaring what sort of person you are.*

For an example of what I mean here, consider writer Ozy Brennan's taxonomy:

> I think a formative moment for any rationalist—our "Uncle Ben shot by the mugger" moment, if you will—is the moment you go "holy shit, everyone in the world is fucking insane." [...]

Now, there are basically two ways you can respond to this.

First, you can say "holy shit, everyone in the world is fucking insane. Therefore, if I adopt the radical new policy of not being fucking insane, I can pick up these giant piles of utility everyone is leaving on the ground, and then I win." [...]

This is the strategy of discovering a hot new stock tip, investing all your money, winning big, and retiring to Maui.

Second, you can say "holy shit, everyone in the world is fucking insane. However, none of them seem to realize that they're insane. By extension, I am probably insane. I should take careful steps to minimize the damage I do." [...]

This is the strategy of discovering a hot new stock tip, realizing that most stock tips are bogus, and not going bankrupt.[35]

According to this sociological hypothesis, people can react to the discovery that "everyone in the world is insane" by adopting the Maui strategy, or they can react by adopting the not-going-bankrupt strategy.

(Note the inevitable comparison to financial markets—the one part of civilization that worked well enough to prompt an economist, Eugene Fama, to come up with the modern notion of efficiency.)

Brennan goes on to say that these two positions form a "dialectic," but that nonetheless, some kinds of people are clearly on the "becoming-sane side of things" while others are more on the "insanity-harm-reduction side of things."

But, speaking first to the basic dichotomy that's being proposed, the whole point of becoming sane is that your beliefs *shouldn't* reflect what sort

---

[35] Brennan, "The World Is Mad" (https://thingofthings.wordpress.com/2015/10/30/the-world-is-mad/).

When I ran a draft of this chapter by Brennan, they said that they basically agree with what I'm saying here, but are thinking about these issues using a different conceptual framework.

of person you are. To the extent you're succeeding, at least, your beliefs should just reflect how the world is.

Good reasoners don't believe that there are goblins in their closets. The ultimate reason for this isn't that goblin-belief is archaic, outmoded, associated with people lost in fantasy worlds, too much like wishful thinking, et cetera. It's just that we opened up our closets and looked and we didn't see any goblins.

The goal is simply to be the sort of person who, in worlds with closet goblins, ends up believing in closet goblins, and in worlds without closet goblins, ends up disbelieving in closet goblins. Avoiding beliefs that sound archaic does relatively little to help you learn that there are goblins in a world where goblins exist, so it does relatively little to establish that there aren't goblins in a world where they don't exist. Examining particular empirical predictions of the goblin hypothesis, on the other hand, *does* provide strong evidence about what world you're in.

To reckon with the discovery that the world is mad, Brennan suggests that we consider the mix of humble and audacious "impulses in our soul" and try to strike the right balance. Perhaps we have some personality traits or biases that dispose us toward believing in goblins, and others that dispose us toward doubting them. On this framing, the heart of the issue is how we can resolve this inner conflict; the heart isn't any question about the behavioral tendencies or physiology of goblins.

This is a central disagreement I have with modest epistemology: modest people end up believing that they live in an inexploitable world *because they're trying to avoid acting like an arrogant kind of person.* Under modest epistemology, you're not supposed to adapt rapidly and without hesitation to the realities of the situation as you observe them, because that would mean trusting *yourself* to assess adequacy levels; but you can't trust yourself, because Dunning-Kruger, et cetera.

The alternative to modest epistemology isn't an *immodest* epistemology where you decide that you're higher status than doctors after all and conclude that you can now invent your own *de novo* medical treatments as a matter of course. The alternative is deciding for yourself whether to trust yourself more than a particular facet of your civilization at this particular time and place, checking the results whenever you can, and building up skill.

When it comes to medicine, I try to keep in mind that anyone whatsoever with more real-world medical experience may have me beat *cold solid* when it comes to any real-world problem. And then I go right on double-checking online to see if I believe what the doctor tells me about whether consuming too much medium-chain triglyceride oil could stress my liver.[36]

In my experience, people who don't viscerally understand Moloch's tool-box and the ubiquitously broken Nash equilibria of real life and how group insanity can arise from intelligent individuals responding to their own incentives tend to unconsciously translate *all* assertions about relative system competence into assertions about relative status. If you don't see systemic competence as rare, or don't see real-world systemic competence as driven by rare instances of correctly aligned incentives, all that's *left* is status. All good and bad output is just driven by good and bad individual people, and to suggest that you'll have better output is to assert that you're individually smarter than everyone else. (This is what status hierarchy feels like from the inside: to perform better is to *be* better.)

On a trip a couple of years ago to talk with the European existential risk community, which has internalized norms from modest epistemology to an even greater extent than the Bay Area community has, I ran into various people who asked questions like, "Why do you and your co-workers at MIRI think you can do better than academia?" (MIRI is the Machine Intelligence Research Institute, the organization I work at.)

I responded that we were a small research institute that sustains itself on individual donors, thereby sidestepping a set of standard organizational demands that collectively create bad incentives for the kind of research we're working on. I described how we had deliberately organized ourselves to steer clear of incentives that discourage long-term substantive research projects, to

---

[36] Answer: this is the opposite of standard theory; she was probably confusing MCT with other forms of saturated fat.

avoid academia's "publish or perish" dynamic, and more generally to navigate around the multiple frontiers of competitiveness where researchers have to spend all their energy competing along those dimensions to get into the best journals.

These are known failure modes that academics routinely complain about, so I wasn't saying anything novel or clever. The point I wanted to emphasize was that it's not enough to say that you want risky long-term research in the abstract; you have to accept that your people won't be at the competitive frontier for journal publications anymore.

The response I got back was something like a divide-by-zero error. Whenever I said "the nonprofit I work at has different incentives that look *prima facie* helpful for solving this set of technical problems," my claim appeared to get parsed as "the nonprofit I work at is *better* (higher status, more authoritative, etc.) than academia."

I think that the people I was talking with had already internalized the mathematical concept of Nash equilibria, but I don't think they were steeped in a no-free-energy microeconomic equilibrium view of all of society where *most of the time* systems end up dumber than the people in them due to multiple layers of terrible incentives, and that this is normal and not at all a surprising state of affairs to suggest. And if you haven't practiced thinking about organizations' comparative advantages from that perspective long enough to make that lens *more cognitively available* than the status comparisons lens, then it makes sense that all talk of relative performance levels between you and doctors, or you and academia, or whatever, will be autoparsed by the easier, more native, more automatic status lens.

Because, come on, do you *really* think you're more authoritative/respectable/qualified/reputable/adept than your doctor about medicine? If you think *that*, won't you start consuming Vitamin C megadoses to treat cancer? And if you're *not* more authoritative/respectable/qualified/reputable/adept than your doctor, then how could you possibly do better by doing Internet research?

(Among most people I know, the relative status feeling frequently gets verbalized in English as "smarter," so if the above paragraph didn't make sense, try replacing the social-status placeholder "authoritative/respectable/etc." with "smarter.")

Again, a lot of the benefit of becoming fluent with this viewpoint is just in having a way of seeing "systems with not-all-that-great outputs," often observed extensively and directly, that can parse into *something* that isn't "Am I higher-status ('smarter,' 'better,' etc.) than the people in the system?"

iii.

I once encountered a case of (honest) misunderstanding from someone who thought that when I cited something as an example of civilizational inadequacy (or as I put it at the time, "People are crazy and the world is mad"), the thing I was trying to argue was that the Great Stagnation was just due to unimpressive/unqualified/low-status ("stupid") scientists.[37] He thought I thought that all we needed to do was take people in our social circle and have them go into biotech, or put scientists through a CFAR unit, and we'd see huge breakthroughs.[38]

"*What?*" I said.

(I was quite surprised.)

"I never said anything like that," I said, after recovering from the shock. "You can't lift a ten-pound weight with one pound of force!"

---

[37] The Great Stagnation is economist Tyler Cowen's hypothesis that declining rates of innovation since the 1970s (excluding information technology, for the most part) have resulted in relative economic stagnation in the developed world.

[38] CFAR, the Center for Applied Rationality, is a nonprofit that applies ideas from cognitive science to everyday problem-solving and decision-making, running workshops for people who want to get better at solving big global problems. MIRI and CFAR are frequent collaborators, and share office space; the organization's original concept came from MIRI's work on rationality.

I went on to say that it's conceivable you could get faster-than-current results if CFAR's annual budget grew 20x, and then they spent four years iterating experimentally on techniques, and then a group of promising biotechnology grad students went through a year of CFAR training...[39]

So another way of thinking about the central question of civilizational inadequacy is that we're trying to assess the *quantity of effort* required to achieve a given level of outperformance. Not "Can it be done?" but "How much work?"

This brings me to the single most obvious notion that correct contrarians grasp, and that people who have vastly overestimated their own competence don't realize: It takes *far* less work to identify the correct expert in a pre-existing dispute between experts, than to make an *original contribution* to any field that is remotely healthy.

I did not work out myself what would be a better policy for the Bank of Japan. I believed the arguments of Scott Sumner, who is not literally mainstream (yet), but whose position is shared by many other economists. I sided with a particular band of contrarian expert economists, based on my attempt to parse the object-level arguments, observing from the sidelines for a while to see who was right about near-term predictions and picking up on what previous experience suggested were strong cues of correct contrarianism.[40]

And so I ended up thinking that I knew better than the Bank of Japan. On the modest view, that's just about as immodest as thinking you can personally advance the state of the art, since who says I ought to be smarter than the Bank of Japan at picking good experts to trust, et cetera?

But in real life, inside a civilization that is often tremendously broken on a systemic level, finding a contrarian expert seeming to shine against an untrustworthy background is *nowhere remotely near* as difficult as becoming that expert yourself. It's the difference between picking which of four runners

---

[39] See also Weinersmith's Law: "*No problem is too hard. Many problems are too fast.*"

[40] E.g., the cry of "Stop ignoring your own carefully gathered experimental evidence, damn it!"

is most likely to win a fifty-kilometer race, and winning a fifty-kilometer race yourself.

Distinguishing a correct contrarian isn't easy in absolute terms. You are still trying to be better than the mainstream in deciding who to trust.[41] For many people, yes, an attempt to identify contrarian experts ends with them trusting faith healers over traditional medicine. But it's still in the range of things that amateurs can do with a reasonable effort, if they've picked up on unusually good epistemology from one source or another.

We live in a sufficiently poorly-functioning world that there are many visibly correct contrarians whose ideas are not yet being implemented in the mainstream, where the authorities who allegedly judge between experts are making errors that appear to me trivial. (And again, by "errors," I mean that these authorities are endorsing factually wrong answers or dominated policies—*not* that they're passing up easy rewards given their incentives.)

In a world like that, you can often know things that the average authority doesn't know... but *not* because you figured it out yourself, in almost every case.

iv.

Going beyond picking the right horse in the race and becoming a horse yourself, inventing your own new personal solution to a civilizational problem, requires a much greater investment of effort.

I did make up my own decision theory—not from a *tabula rasa*, but still to my own recipe. But events like that should be *rare* in a given person's life. Logical counterfactuals in decision theory are one of my *few* major contributions to an existing academic field, and my early thoughts on this

---

[41] Though, to be clear, the mainstream isn't *actually* deciding who to trust. It's picking winners by some other criterion that on a good day is not totally uncorrelated with trustworthiness.

topic were quickly improved on by others.[42] And that was a significant life event, not the sort of thing I believe I've done every month.

Above all, reaching the true frontier requires *picking your battles*.

Computer security professionals don't attack systems by picking one particular function and saying, "Now I shall find a way to exploit these exact 20 lines of code!" Most lines of code in a system don't provide exploits no matter how hard you look at them. In a large enough system, there are rare lines of code that are exceptions to this general rule, and sometimes you can be the first to find them. But if we think about a random section of code, the base rate of exploitability is extremely low—except in *really, really bad code* that nobody looked at from a security standpoint in the first place.

Thinking that you've searched a large system and found one new exploit is one thing. Thinking that you can exploit arbitrary lines of code is quite another.

No matter how broken academia is, no one can improve on arbitrary parts of the modern academic edifice. My own base frequency for seeing scholarship that I think I can improve upon is "almost never," outside of some academic subfields dealing with the equivalent of "unusually bad code." But don't expect bad code to be guarding vaults of gleaming gold in a form that other people value, except with a very low base rate. There do tend to be real locks on the energy-containing vaults not already emptied... *almost* (but not quite) all of the time.

Similarly, you do not generate a good startup idea by taking some random activity, and then talking yourself into believing you can do it better than existing companies. Even where the current way of doing things seems bad, and even when you really do know a better way, 99 times out of 100 you will not be able to make money by knowing better. If somebody else makes money on a solution to that particular problem, they'll do it using rare resources or

---

[42] In particular, Wei Dai came up with updatelessness, yielding the earliest version of what's now called functional decision theory. See Soares and Levinstein's "Cheating Death in Damascus" (https://intelligence.org/files/DeathInDamascus.pdf) for a description.

skills that you don't have—including the skill of being super-charismatic and getting tons of venture capital to do it.

To believe you have a good startup idea is to say, "Unlike the typical 99 cases, in this particular anomalous and unusual case, I think I *can* make a profit by knowing a better way."

The anomaly doesn't have to be some super-unusual skill possessed by you alone in all the world. That would be a question that always returned "No," a blind set of goggles. Having an unusually good idea might work well enough to be worth trying, if you think you can standardly solve the other standard startup problems. I'm merely emphasizing that to find a rare startup idea that is *exploitable* in dollars, you will have to *scan and keep scanning*, not pursue the first "X is broken and maybe I can fix it!" thought that pops into your head.

To win, choose winnable battles; await the rare *anomalous* case of, "Oh wait, that could work."

v.

In 2014, I experimentally put together my own ketogenic meal replacement drink via several weeks of research, plus months of empirical tweaking, to see if it could help me with long-term weight normalization.

In that case, I did not get to pick my battleground.

And yet even so, I still tried to design my own recipe. Why? It seems I must have thought I could do better than the best ketogenic liquid-food recipes that had ever before been tried, as of 2014. Why would I believe I could do the best of anyone who's yet tried, when I couldn't pick my battle?

Well, because I looked up previous ketogenic Soylent recipes, and they used standard multivitamin powders containing, e.g., way too much manganese and the wrong form of selenium. (You get all the manganese you need from ordinary drinking water, if it hasn't been distilled or bottled. Excess amounts may be *neurotoxic*. One of the leading hypotheses for why multivitamins aren't found to produce net health improvement, despite having many individual components found to be helpful, is that multivitamins contain 100% of the US RDA of manganese. Similarly, if a multivitamin includes sodium selenite instead of, e.g., se-methyl-selenocysteine, it's the equivalent of handing you a lump of charcoal and saying, "You're a carbon-based lifeform; this has carbon in it, right?")

Just for the sake of grim amusement, I also looked up my civilization's medically standard ketogenic dietary options—e.g., for epileptic children. As expected, they were far worse than the amateur Soylent-inspired recipes. They didn't even contain medium-chain triglycerides, which your liver turns directly into ketones. (MCT is academically recommended, though not commercially standard, as the basis for maintaining ketosis in epileptic children.) Instead the retail dietary options for epileptic children involved mostly soybean oil, of which it has been said, "Why not just shoot them?"

Even when we can't pick our battleground, sometimes the most advanced weapon on offer turns out to be a broken stick and it's worth the time to carve a handaxe.

… But even then, I didn't try to synthesize my own dietary *theory* from scratch. There is nothing I believe about how human metabolism works that's unique or original to me. Not a single element of my homemade Ketosoylent was based on my personal, private theory of how *any* of the micronutrients worked. Who am I to think I understand Vitamin D3 better than everyone else in the world?

The Ketosoylent didn't work for long-term weight normalization, alas— the same result as all other replicated experiments on trying to long-term-normalize weight via putting different things inside your mouth. (The Shangri-La Diet I mentioned at the start of this book didn't work for me either.)

So it goes. I mention the Ketosoylent because it's the most complicated thing I've tried to do *without* tons of experience in a domain and *without* being able to pick my battles.

In the simpler and happier case of treating Brienne's Seasonal Affective Disorder, I again didn't get to pick the battleground; but SAD has received far less scientific attention to date than obesity. And success there again didn't involve coming up with an amazing new model of SAD. It's not weird and private knowledge that sufficiently bright light might cure SAD. The Sun is known to work almost all the time.

So a realistic lifetime of trying to adapt yourself to a broken civilization looks like:

- 0-2 lifetime instances of answering "Yes" to "Can I substantially improve on my civilization's current knowledge *if I put years into the attempt?*" A few people, but not many, will answer "Yes" to enough instances of this question to count on the fingers of both hands. Moving on to your toes indicates that you are a crackpot.

- Once per year or thereabouts, an answer of "Yes" to "Can I generate a synthesis of existing correct contrarianism which will beat my current civilization's next-best alternative, for just myself (i.e., without trying to solve the further problems of widespread adoption), after a few weeks' research and a bunch of testing and occasionally asking for help?" (See my experiments with ketogenic diets and SAD treatment; also what you would do to generate or judge a startup idea that wasn't based on a hard science problem.)

- *Many* cases of trying to pick a previously existing side in a running dispute between experts, if you think that you can follow the object-level arguments reasonably well and there are strong meta-level cues that you can identify.

The accumulation of many judgments of the latter kind is where you get the fuel for many small day-to-day decisions (e.g., about what to eat), and much of your ability to do larger things (like solving a medical problem after going through the medical system has proved fruitless, or executing well on a startup).

vi.

A few final pieces of advice on everyday thinking about inadequacy:

When it comes to estimating the competence of some aspect of civilization, especially relative to your own competence, try to update hard on your experiences of failure and success. One data point is a hell of a lot better than zero data points.

Worrying about how one data point is "just an anecdote" can make sense if you've already collected thirty data points. On the other hand, when you previously just had a lot of prior reasoning, or you were previously trying to generalize from other people's not-quite-similar experiences, and then you collide directly with reality for the first time, one data point is *huge*.

If you do accidentally update too far, you can always re-update later when you have more data points. So update hard on each occasion, and take care not to flush any new observation down the toilet.

Oh, and bet. Bet on everything. Bet real money. It helps a lot with learning.

I once bet $25 at even odds against the eventual discovery of the Higgs boson—after 90% of the possible mass range had been experimentally eliminated, because I had the impression from reading diatribes against string theory that modern theoretical physics might not be solid enough to predict a qualitatively new kind of particle with prior odds greater than 9:1.

When the Higgs boson was discovered inside the remaining 10% interval of possible energies, I said, "Gosh, I guess they *can* predict that sort of thing with prior probability greater than 90%," updated strongly in favor of the credibility of things like dark matter and dark energy, and then didn't make any more bets like that.

I made a mistake; and I bet on it. This let me *experience* the mistake in a way that helped me better learn from it. When you're thinking about large, messy phenomena like "the adequacy of human civilization at understanding nutrition," it's easy to get caught up in plausible-sounding stories and never quite get around to running the experiment. Run experiments; place bets; say *oops*. Anything less is an act of self-sabotage.

5. Blind Empiricism

The thesis that needs to be contrasted with modesty is not the assertion that everyone can beat their civilization all the time. It's not that we should be *the sort of person* who sees the world as mad and pursues the strategy of believing a hot stock tip and investing everything.

It's just that it's *okay* to reason about the particulars of where civilization might be inadequate, *okay* to end up believing that you can state a better monetary policy than the Bank of Japan is implementing, *okay* to check that against observation whenever you get the chance, and okay to update on the results in *either* direction. It's okay to act on a model of what you think the rest of the world is good at, and for this model to be sensitive to the specifics of different cases.

Why might this *not* be okay?

It could be that "acting on a model" is suspect, at least when it comes to complicated macrophenomena. Consider Isaiah Berlin's distinction between "hedgehogs" (who rely more on theories, models, global beliefs) and "foxes" (who rely more on data, observations, local beliefs). Many people I know see the fox's mindset as more admirable than the hedgehog's, on the basis that it has greater immunity to fantasy and dogmatism. And Philip Tetlock's research has shown that political experts who rely heavily on simple overarching theories—the kind of people who use the word "moreover" more often than "however"—perform substantially worse on average in forecasting tasks.[43]

Or perhaps the suspect part is when models are "sensitive to the specifics of different cases." In a 2002 study, Buehler, Griffin, and Ross asked a group of experimental subjects to provide lots of details about their Christmas shopping plans: where, when, and how. On average, this experimental

---

[43] See Philip Tetlock, "Why Foxes Are Better Forecasters Than Hedgehogs" (https://long-now.org/seminars/02007/jan/26/why-foxes-are-better-forecasters-than-hedgehogs/).

group expected to finish shopping more than a week before Christmas. Another group was simply asked when they expected to finish their Christmas shopping, with an average response of 4 days. Both groups finished an average of 3 days before Christmas. Similarly, students who expected to finish their assignments 10 days before deadline actually finished one day before deadline; and when asked when they had previously completed similar tasks, replied, "one day before deadline." This suggests that taking the *outside view* is an effective response to the planning fallacy: rather than trying to predict how many hiccups and delays your plans will run into by reflecting in detail on each plan's particulars (the "inside view"), you can do better by just guessing that your future plans will work out roughly as well as your past plans.

As stated, these can be perfectly good debiasing measures. I worry, however, that many people end up misusing and overapplying the "outside view" concept very soon after they learn about it, and that a lot of people tie too much of their mental conception of what good reasoning looks like to the stereotype of the humble empiricist fox. I recently noticed this as a common thread running through three conversations I had.

I am not able to recount these conversations in a way that does justice to the people I spoke to, so please treat my recounting as an unfair and biased illustration of relevant ideas, rather than as a neutral recitation of the facts. My goal is to illustrate the kinds of reasoning patterns I think are causing epistemic harm: to point to some canaries in the coal mine, and to be clear that when I talk about modesty I'm not just talking about Hal Finney's majoritarianism or the explicit belief in civilizational adequacy.

i.

Conversation 1 was about the importance of writing code to test AI ideas. I suggested that when people tried writing code to test an idea I considered important, I wanted to see the code in advance of the experiment, or without being told the result, to see if I could predict the outcome correctly.

I got pushback against this, which surprised me; so I replied that my having a chance to make advance experimental predictions was important, for two reasons.

First, I thought it was important to develop a skill and methodology of predicting "these sorts of things" in advance, because past a certain level of development when working with smarter-than-human AI, if you can't see the bullets coming in advance of the experiment, the experiment kills you. This being the case, I needed to test this skill as much as possible, which meant trying to make experimental predictions in advance so I could put myself on trial.

Second, if I could predict the results correctly, it meant that the experiments weren't saying anything I hadn't figured out through past experience and theorizing. I was worried that somebody might take a result I considered an obvious prediction under my current views and say that it was evidence against my theory or methodology, since both often get misunderstood.[44] If you want to use experiment to show that a certain theory or methodology fails, you need to give advocates of the theory/methodology a chance to say beforehand what they think they predict, so the prediction is on the record and neither side can move the goalposts.

---

[44] As an example, my conception of the reward hacking problem for reinforcement learning systems is that below certain capability thresholds, making the system smarter will often produce increasingly helpful behavior, assuming the rewards are a moderately good proxy for the actual objectives we want the system to achieve. The problem of the system exploiting loopholes and finding ways to maximize rewards in undesirable ways is mainly introduced when the system's resourcefulness is great enough, and its policy search space large enough, that operators can't foresee even in broad strokes what the reward-maximizing strategies are likely to look like. If this idea gets rounded off to just "making an RL system smarter will always reduce its alignment with the operator's goal," however, then a researcher will misconstrue what counts as evidence for or against prioritizing reward hacking research.

And there are many other cases where ideas in AI alignment tend to be misunderstood, largely because "AI" calls to mind present-day applications. It's certainly possible to run useful experiments with present-day software to learn things about future AGI systems, but "see, this hill-climbing algorithm doesn't exhibit the behavior you predicted for highly capable Bayesian reasoners" will usually reflect a misconception about what the concept of Bayesian reasoning is doing in AGI alignment theory.

And I still got pushback, from a MIRI supporter with a strong technical background; so I conversed further.

I now suspect that—at least this is what I think was going on—their mental contrast between empiricism and theoreticism was so strong that they thought it was unsafe to have a theory *at all.* That having a theory made you a bad hedgehog with one big idea instead of a good fox who has lots of little observations. That the dichotomy was between making an advance prediction *instead of doing the experiment,* versus doing the experiment *without any advance prediction.* Like, I suspect that every time I talked about "making a prediction" they heard "making a prediction instead of doing an experiment" or "clinging to what you predict will happen and ignoring the experiment."

I can see how this kind of outlook would develop. The policy of making predictions to *test* your understanding, to put it on trial, presupposes that you can execute the "quickly say *oops* and abandon your old belief" technique, so that you can employ it if the prediction turns out to be wrong. To the extent that "quickly say *oops* and abandon your old belief" is something the vast majority of people fail at, maybe on an individual level it's better for people to try to be pure foxes and only collect observations and try not to have any big theories. Maybe the average cognitive use case is that if you have a big theory and observation contradicts it, you will find some way to keep the big theory and thereby doom yourself. (The "Mistakes Were Made, But Not By Me" effect.)

But from my perspective, there's no choice. You just have to master "say *oops*" so that you can have theories and make experimental predictions. Even on a strictly empiricist level, if you aren't allowed to have models and you don't make your predictions in advance, you learn less. An empiricist of that sort can only learn surface generalizations about whether this phenomenon superficially "looks like" that phenomenon, rather than building causal models and putting them on trial.

ii.

Conversation 2 was about a web application under development, and it went something like this.

> **STARTUP FOUNDER 1:** I want to get (primitive version of product) in front of users as fast as possible, to see whether they want to use it or not.

> **ELIEZER:** I predict users will not want to use this version.

> **FOUNDER 1:** Well, from the things I've read about startups, it's important to test as early as possible whether users like your product, and not to overengineer things.

> **ELIEZER:** The concept of a "minimum viable product" isn't the minimum product that compiles. It's the least product that is the *best tool in the world* for some particular task or workflow. If you don't have an MVP in that sense, of course the users won't switch. So you don't have a testable hypothesis. So you're not really learning anything when the users don't want to use your product.[45]

> **FOUNDER 1:** No battle plan survives contact with reality. The important thing is just to get the product in front of users as quickly as possible, so you can see what they think. That's why I'm disheartened that (group of users) did not want to use (early version of product).

> **ELIEZER:** This reminds me of a conversation I had about AI twice in the last month. Two separate people were claiming that we would only learn things empirically by experimenting, and I said

---

[45] I did not say this then, but I should have: Overengineering is when you try to make everything look pretty, or add additional cool features that you think the users will like... not when you try to put in the key core features that are necessary for your product to be the best tool the user has ever seen for at least one workflow.

that in cases like that, I wanted to see the experiment description in advance so I could make advance predictions and put on trial my ability to foresee things without being hit over the head by them.

In both of those conversations I had a very hard time conveying the idea, "Just because I have a theory does not mean I have to be insensitive to evidence; the evidence *tests* the theory, potentially falsifies the theory, but for that to work you need to make experimental predictions in advance." I think I could have told you in advance that (group of users) would not want to use (early version of product), because (group of users) is trying to accomplish (task 1) and this version of the product is not the best available tool they'll have seen for doing (task 1).

I can't convey it very well with all the details redacted, but the impression I got was that the message of "distrust theorizing" had become so strong that Founder 1 had stopped trying to model users in detail and thought it was futile to make an advance prediction. But if you can't model users in detail, you can't think in terms of workflows and tasks that users are trying to accomplish, or at what point you become visibly the best tool the user has ever encountered to accomplish some particular workflow (the minimum viable product). The alternative, from what I could see, was to think in terms of "features" and that as soon as possible you would show the product to the user and see if they wanted that subset of features.

There's a version of this hypothesis which does make sense, which is that when you have the minimum compilable product that it is physically possible for a user to interact with, you can ask one of your friends to sit down in front of it, you can *make a prediction* about what parts they will dislike or find difficult, and then you can see if your prediction is correct. Maybe your product actually fails much earlier than you expect.

But this is not like getting early users to voluntarily adopt your product. This is about observing, as early as possible, how volunteers react to unviable versions of your product, so you know what needs fixing earliest or whether the exposed parts of your theory are holding up so far.

It really looks to me like the modest reactions to certain types of overconfidence or error are taken by many believers in modesty to mean, in practice, that theories just get you into trouble; that you can either make predictions *or* look at reality, but not both.

iii.

Conversation 3 was with Startup Founder 2, a member of the effective altruism community who was making Material Objects—I'll call them "Snowshoes"—who had remarked that modern venture capital was only interested in 1000x returns and not 20x returns.

I asked why he wasn't trying for 1000x returns with his current company selling Snowshoes—was that more annoyance/work than he wanted to undertake?

He replied that most companies in a related industry, Flippers, weren't that large, and it seemed to him that based on the outside view, he shouldn't expect his company to become larger than the average company in the Flippers industry. He asked if I was telling him to try being more confident.

I responded that, no, the thing I wanted him to think was orthogonal to modesty versus confidence. I observed that the customer use case for Flippers was actually quite different from Snowshoes, and asked him if he'd considered how many uses of Previous Snowshoes in the world would, in fact, benefit from being replaced by the more developed version of Snowshoes he was making.

He said that this seemed to him too much like optimism or fantasy, compared to asking what his company had to do next.

I had asked about how customers would benefit from new and improved Snowshoes because my background model says that startups are more likely to succeed if they provide real economic value—value of the kind that Danslist would provide over Craigslist if Danslist succeeded, and of the kind that Craigslist provides over newspaper classifieds. Getting people to actually buy your product, of course, is a separate question from whether it would provide real value of that kind. And there's an obvious failure mode where you're in love with your product and you overestimate the product's value or underestimate the costs to the user. There's an obvious failure mode where you just look at the real economic value and get all cheerful about that, without asking the further necessary question of how many decisionmakers *will* choose to use your product; or whether your marketing message is either opaque or easily faked; or whether any competitors will get there first if they see you being successful early on; or whether you could defend a price premium in the face of competition. But the question of real economic value seems to me to be one of the factors going into a startup's odds of succeeding— Craigslist's success is in part explained by the actual benefit buyers and sellers derive from the existence of Craigslist—and worth factoring out before discussing purchaser decisionmaking and value-capturing questions.[46]

It wasn't that I was trying to get Founder 2 to be more optimistic (though I did think, given his Snowshoes product, that he ought to at least *try* to be more ambitious). It was that it looked to me like the outside view was shutting down his causal model of how and why people might use his product, and substituting, "Just try to build your Snowshoes and see what happens, and at best don't expect to succeed more than the average company in a related industry." But I don't think you can get so far as even the *average* surviving company, unless you have a causal model (the dreaded inside view) of where your company is supposed to go and what resources are required to get there.

I was asking, "What level do you want to grow to? What needs to be done for your company to grow that much? What's the obstacle to taking the next step?" And... I think it felt immodest to him to claim that his company could

---

[46]And a startup founder definitely needs to ask that question and answer it before they go out and try to raise venture capital from investors who are looking for 1000x returns. Don't discount your company's case before it starts. They'll do that for you.

grow to a given level; so he thought only in terms of things he knew he could try, forward-chaining from where he was rather than backward-chaining from where he wanted to go, because that way he didn't need to immodestly think about succeeding at a particular level, or endorse an inside view of a particular pathway.

I think the details of his business plan had the same outside-view problem. In the Flippers industry, two common versions of Flippers that were sold were Deluxe Flippers and Basic Flippers. Deluxe Flippers were basically preassembled Basic Flippers, and Deluxe Flippers sold for a much higher premium than Basic Flippers even though it was easy to assemble them.

We were talking about a potential variation of his Snowshoes, and he said that it would be too expensive to ship a Deluxe version, but not worth it to ship a Basic version, given the average premiums the outside view said these products could command.

I asked him *why*, in the Flippers industry, Deluxe sold for such a premium over Basic when it was so easy to assemble Basic into Deluxe. Why was this price premium being maintained?

He suggested that maybe people really valued the last little bit of convenience from buying Deluxe instead of Basic.

I suggested that in this large industry of slightly differentiated Flippers, maybe a lot of price-sensitive consumers bought only Basic versions, meaning that the few Deluxe buyers were price-insensitive. I then observed again that the best use case for his product was quite different from the standard use case in the Flipper industry, and that he didn't have much direct competition. I suggested that, for his customers that weren't otherwise customers in the Flippers industry, it wouldn't make much of a difference to his pricing power whether he sold Deluxe or the much easier to ship Basic version.

And I remarked that it seemed to me unwise in general to look at a *mysterious* pricing premium, and assume that you could get that premium. You couldn't just look at average Deluxe prices and assume you could get them. Generally speaking, this indicates some sort of rent or market barrier; and where there is a stream of rent, there will be walls built to exclude other people from drinking from the stream. Maybe the high Deluxe prices meant that Deluxe consumers were hard to market to, or very unlikely to switch providers. You couldn't just take the outside view of what Deluxe products tended to sell like.

He replied that he didn't think it was wise to say that you had to fully understand every part of the market before you could do anything; especially because, if you had to understand why Deluxe products sold at a premium, it would be so easy to just make up an explanation.

Again I understand where he was coming from, in terms of the average cognitive use case. When I try to explain a phenomenon, I'm also implicitly relying on my ability to use a technique like "don't even start to rationalize," which is a skill that I started practicing at age 15 and that took me a decade to hone to a reliable and productive form. I also used the "notice when you're confused about something" technique to ask the question, and a number of other mental habits and techniques for explaining mysterious phenomena—for starters, "detecting goodness of fit" (see whether the explanation feels "forced") and "try further critiquing the answer." Maybe there's no point in trying to explain why Deluxe products sell at a premium to Basic products, if you don't already have a lot of cognitive technique for not coming up with terrible explanations for mysteries, along with enough economics background to know which things are important mysteries in the first place, which explanations are plausible, and so on.

But at the same time, it seems to me that there is a learnable skill here, one that entrepreneurs and venture capitalists at least *have* to learn if they want to succeed on purpose instead of by luck.

One needs to be able to identify mysterious pricing and sales phenomena, read enough economics to speak the right simplicity language for one's hypotheses, and then not come up with terrible rationalizations. One needs to learn the key answers for how the challenged industry works, which means that one needs to have explicit hypotheses that one can test as early as possible.

Otherwise you're... not quite doomed *per se*, but from the perspective of somebody like me, there will be ten of you with bad ideas for every one of you that happens to have a good idea. And the people that do have good ideas will not really understand what human problems they are addressing, what their potential users' relevant motivations are, or what are their critical obstacles to success.

Given that analysis of ideas takes place on the level it does, I can understand why people would say that it's futile to try to analyze ideas, or that teams rather than ideas are important. I'm not saying that either entrepreneurs or venture capitalists could, by an effort of will, suddenly become great at analyzing ideas. But it seems to me that the outside view concept, along with the Fox=Good/Hedgehog=Bad, Observation=Good/Theory=Bad messages—including the related misunderstanding of MVP as "just build something and show it to users"—are preventing people from even starting to develop those skills. At least, my observation is that some people go too far in their skepticism of model-building.[47]

Maybe there's a valley of bad rationality here and the injunction to not try to have theories or causal models or preconceived predictions is protective against entering it. But first, if it came down to only those alternatives, I'd frankly rather see twenty aspiring rationalists fail painfully until one of them develops the required skills, rather than have nobody with those skills. And second, god damn it, there has to be a better way.

iv.

In situations that are drawn from a barrel of causally similar situations, where human optimism runs rampant and unforeseen troubles are common, the

---

[47] As Tetlock puts it in a discussion of the limitations of the fox/hedgehog model in the book *Superforecasting*: "Models are supposed to simplify things, which is why even the best are flawed. But they're necessary. Our minds are full of models. We couldn't function without them. And we often function pretty well because some of our models are decent approximations of reality."

outside view beats the inside view. But in novel situations where causal mechanisms differ, the outside view fails—there may not be relevantly similar cases, or it may be ambiguous which similar-looking cases are the right ones to look at.

Where two sides disagree, this can lead to *reference class tennis*—both parties get stuck insisting that their own "outside view" is the correct one, based on diverging intuitions about what similarities are relevant. If it isn't clear what the set of "similar historical cases" is, or what conclusions we should draw from those cases, then we're forced to use an inside view—thinking about the causal process to distinguish relevant similarities from irrelevant ones.

You shouldn't avoid outside-view-style reasoning in cases where it looks likely to work, like when planning your Christmas shopping. But in many contexts, the outside view simply can't compete with a good theory.

Intellectual progress on the whole has usually been the process of moving from surface-level resemblances to more technical understandings of particulars. Extreme examples of this are common in science and engineering: the deep causal models of the world that allowed humans to plot the trajectory of the first moon rocket before launch, for example, or that allow us to verify that a computer chip will work before it's ever manufactured.

Where items in a reference class differ causally in more ways than two Christmas shopping trips you've planned or two university essays you've written, or where there's temptation to cherry-pick the reference class of things you consider "similar" to the phenomenon in question, or where the particular biases underlying the planning fallacy just aren't a factor, you're often better off doing the hard cognitive labor of building, testing, and acting on models of how phenomena actually work, even if those models are very rough and very uncertain, or admit of many exceptions and nuances. And, of course, during and after the construction of the model, you have to look at the data. You still need fox-style attention to detail—and you certainly need empiricism.

The idea isn't, "Be a hedgehog, not a fox." The idea is rather: developing accurate beliefs requires both observation of the data *and* the development of models and theories that can be tested by the data. In most cases, there's no real alternative to sticking your neck out, even knowing that reality might surprise you and chop off your head.

6. Against Modest Epistemology

Modest epistemology doesn't need to reflect a skepticism about causal models as such. It can manifest instead as a wariness about putting weight down on *one's own* causal models, as opposed to others'.

In 1976, Robert Aumann demonstrated that two ideal Bayesian reasoners with the same priors cannot have common knowledge of a disagreement. Tyler Cowen and Robin Hanson have extended this result, establishing that even under various weaker assumptions, something has to go *wrong* in order for two agents with the same priors to get stuck in a disagreement.[48] If you and a trusted peer don't converge on identical beliefs once you have a full understanding of one another's positions, at least one of you must be making *some* kind of mistake.

If we were fully rational (and fully honest), then we would always eventually reach consensus on questions of fact. To become more rational, then, shouldn't we set aside our claims to special knowledge or insight and modestly profess that, really, we're all in the same boat?

When I'm trying to sort out questions like these, I often find it useful to start with a related question: "If I were building a brain from scratch, would I have it act this way?"

If I were building a brain and I expected it to have some non-fatal flaws in its cognitive algorithms, I expect that I would have it spend some of its time using those flawed reasoning algorithms to think about the world; and I would have it spend some of its time using those same flawed reasoning algorithms to better understand its reasoning algorithms. I would have the brain spend most of its time on object-level problems, while spending some

---

[48] See Cowen and Hanson, "Are Disagreements Honest?" (https://mason.gmu.edu/ rhanson/deceive.pdf).

time trying to build better meta-level models of its own cognition and how its cognition relates to its apparent success or failure on object-level problems.

If the thinker is dealing with a foreign cognitive system, I would want the thinker to try to model the other agent's thinking and *predict* the degree of accuracy this system will have. However, the thinker should also record the *empirical* outcomes, and notice if the other agent's accuracy is more or less than expected. If particular agents are more often correct than its model predicts, the system should recalibrate its estimates so that it won't be predictably mistaken in a known direction.

In other words, I would want the brain to reason about brains in pretty much the same way it reasons about other things in the world. And in practice, I suspect that the way I think, and the way I'd advise people in the real world to think, works very much like that:

- Try to spend most of your time thinking about the object level. If you're spending more of your time thinking about your own reasoning ability and competence than you spend thinking about Japan's interest rates and NGDP, or competing omega-6 vs. omega-3 metabolic pathways, you're taking your eye off the ball.

- Less than a majority of the time: Think about how reliable authorities seem to be and should be expected to be, and how reliable you are— using your own brain to think about the reliability and failure modes of brains, since that's what you've got. Try to be evenhanded in how you evaluate your own brain's *specific* failures versus the *specific* failures of other brains.[49] While doing this, *take your own meta-reasoning at face value.*

- … and then next, theoretically, should come the meta-meta level, considered yet more rarely. But I don't think it's necessary to develop

---

[49]This doesn't mean the net estimate of who's wrong comes out 50-50. It means that if you rationalized last Tuesday then you expect yourself to rationalize this Tuesday, if you would expect the same thing of someone else after seeing the same evidence.

special skills for meta-meta reasoning. You just apply the skills you already learned on the meta level to correct your own brain, and go on applying them *while* you happen to be meta-reasoning about who should be trusted, about degrees of reliability, and so on. Anything you've already learned about reasoning should automatically be applied to how you reason about meta-reasoning.[50]

- Consider whether someone else might be a better meta-reasoner than you, and hence that it might *not* be wise to take your own meta-reasoning at face value when disagreeing with them, *if you have been given strong local evidence to this effect.*

That probably sounded terribly abstract, but in practice it means that everything plays out in what I'd consider to be the obvious intuitive fashion.

i.

Once upon a time, my colleague Anna Salamon and I had a disagreement. I thought—this sounds really stupid in retrospect, but keep in mind that this was without benefit of hindsight—I thought that the best way to teach people about detaching from sunk costs was to write a script for local *Less Wrong* meetup leaders to carry out exercises, thus enabling all such meetups to be taught how to avoid sunk costs. We spent a couple of months trying to write this sunk costs unit, though a lot of that was (as I conceived of it) an up-front cost to figure out the basics of how a unit should work at all.

Anna was against this. Anna thought we should not try to carefully write a unit. Anna thought we should just find some volunteers and improvise a sunk costs teaching session and see what happened.

I explained that I wasn't starting out with the hypothesis that you *could* successfully teach anti-sunk-cost reasoning by improvisation, and therefore I

---

[50] And then the recursion stops here, first because we already went in a loop, and second because in practice nothing novel happens after the third level of any infinite recursion.

didn't think I'd learn much from observing the improvised version fail. This may sound less stupid if you consider that I was accustomed to writing many things, most of which never worked or accomplished anything, and a very few of which people paid attention to and mentioned later, and that it had taken me years of writing practice to get even that far. And so, to me, negative examples seemed too common to be valuable. The literature was full of failed attempts to correct for cognitive biases—would one more example of that really help?

I tried to carefully craft a sunk costs unit that would rise above the standard level (which was failure), so that we would actually learn something when we ran it (I reasoned). I also didn't think up-front that it would be two months to craft; the completion time just kept extending gradually—beware the planning fallacy!—and then at some point we figured we had to run what we had.

As read by one of the more experienced meetup leaders, the script did not work. It was, by my standards, a miserable failure.

Here are three lessons I learned from that experiment.

The first lesson is to not carefully craft anything that it was possible to *literally* just improvise and test immediately in its improvised version, ever. Even if the minimum improvisable product won't be representative of the real version. Even if you already expect the current version to fail. You *don't know* what you'll learn from trying the improvised version.[51]

The second lesson was that my model of teaching rationality by producing units for consumption at meetups wasn't going to work, and we'd need to go with Anna's approach of training teachers who could fail on more rapid cycles, and running centralized workshops using those teachers.

The third thing I learned was to avoid disagreeing with Anna Salamon in cases where we would have common knowledge of the disagreement.

What I learned wasn't quite as simple as, "Anna is often right." Eliezer is also often right.

---

[51] Chapter 22 of my *Harry Potter* fanfiction, *Harry Potter and the Methods of Rationality* (https://hpmor.com), was written after I learned this lesson.

What I learned wasn't as simple as, "When Anna and Eliezer disagree, Anna is more likely to be right." We've had a lot of first-order disagreements and I haven't particularly been tracking whose first-order guesses are right more often.

But the case above wasn't a first-order disagreement. I had presented my reasons, and Anna had understood and internalized them and given her advice, and *then* I had guessed that in a situation like this I was more likely to be right. So what I learned is, "Anna is sometimes right *even when my usual meta-reasoning heuristics say otherwise*," which was the real surprise and the first point at which something like an extra push toward agreement is additionally necessary.

It doesn't particularly surprise me if a physicist knows more about photons than I do; that's a case in which my usual meta-reasoning already predicts the physicist will do better, and I don't need any additional nudge to correct it. What I learned from that significant multi-month example was that my *meta-rationality*—my ability to judge which of two people is thinking more clearly and better integrating the evidence in a given context—was not particularly better than Anna's meta-rationality. And that meant the conditions for something like Cowen and Hanson's extension of Aumann's agreement theorem were actually being fulfilled. Not pretend ought-to-be fulfilled, but actually fulfilled.

Could adopting modest epistemology in general have helped me get the right answer in this case? The versions of modest epistemology I hear about usually involve deference to the majority view, to the academic mainstream, or to publicly recognized elite opinion. Anna wasn't a majority; there were two of us, and nobody else in particular was party to the argument. Neither of us were part of a mainstream. And at the point in time where Anna and I had that disagreement, any outsider would have thought that Eliezer Yudkowsky had the more impressive track record at teaching rationality. Anna wasn't yet heading CFAR. Any advice to follow track records, to trust externally observable eliteness in order to avoid the temptation to overconfidence, would have favored listening to Yudkowsky over Salamon—that's part of the reason I trusted myself over her in the first place! And then I was wrong anyway, because in real life that is allowed to happen even when one person has more externally observable status than another.

Whereupon I began to hesitate to disagree with Anna, and hesitate even more if she had heard out my reasons and yet still disagreed with me.

I extend a similar courtesy to Nick Bostrom, who recognized the importance of AI alignment three years before I did (as I discovered afterwards, reading through one of his papers). Once upon a time I thought Nick Bostrom couldn't possibly get anything done in academia, and that he was staying in academia for bad reasons. After I saw Nick Bostrom successfully found his own research institute doing interesting things, I concluded that I was wrong to think Bostrom should leave academia—and also *meta-wrong* to have been so confident while disagreeing with Nick Bostrom. I still think that oracle AI (limiting AI systems to only answer questions) isn't a particularly useful concept to study in AI alignment, but every now and then I dust off the idea and check to see how much sense oracles currently make to me, because Nick Bostrom thinks they might be important even after knowing that I'm more skeptical.

There are people who think we all ought to behave this way toward each other as a matter of course. They reason:

a) on average, we can't all be more meta-rational than average; and

b) you can't trust the reasoning you use to think you're more meta-rational than average. After all, due to Dunning-Kruger, a young-Earth creationist will also think they have plausible reasoning for why they're more meta-rational than average.

… Whereas it seems to me that if I lived in a world where the average person on the street corner were Anna Salamon or Nick Bostrom, the world would look extremely different from how it actually does.

… And from the fact that you're reading this at all, I expect that if the average person on the street corner were *you*, the world would again look extremely different from how it actually does.

(In the event that this book is ever read by more than 30% of Earth's population, I withdraw the above claim.)

ii.

I once poked at someone who seemed to be arguing for a view in line with modest epistemology, nagging them to try to formalize their epistemology. They suggested that we all treat ourselves as having a black box receiver (our brain) which produces a signal (opinions), and treat other people as having other black boxes producing other signals. And we all received our black boxes at random—from an anthropic perspective of some kind, where we think we have an equal chance of being any observer. So we can't start out by believing that our signal is likely to be more accurate than average.

But I don't think of myself as having started out with the *a priori* assumption that I have a better black box. I learned about processes for producing good judgments, like Bayes's Rule, and this let me observe when other people violated Bayes's Rule, and try to keep to it myself. Or I read about sunk cost effects, and developed techniques for avoiding sunk costs so I can abandon bad beliefs faster. After having made observations about people's real-world performance and invested a lot of time and effort into getting better, I expect some degree of outperformance relative to people who haven't made similar investments.

To which the modest reply is: "Oh, but any crackpot could say that their personal epistemology is better because it's based on a bunch of stuff that they think is cool. What makes you different?"

Or as someone advocating what I took to be modesty recently said to me, after I explained why I thought it was sometimes okay to give yourself the discretion to disagree with mainstream expertise when the mainstream seems to be screwing up, in exactly the following words: "But then what do you say to the Republican?"

Or as Ozy Brennan puts it, in dialogue form:

BECOMING SANE SIDE: "Hey! Guys! I found out how to take over the world using only the power of my mind and a toothpick."

HARM REDUCTION SIDE: "You can't do that. Nobody's done that before."

BECOMING SANE SIDE: "Of course they didn't, they were completely irrational."

HARM REDUCTION SIDE: "But they thought they were rational, too."

BECOMING SANE SIDE: "The difference is that I'm right."

HARM REDUCTION SIDE: "They thought that, too!"

This question, "But what if a crackpot said the same thing?", I've never heard formalized—though it seems clearly central to the modest paradigm.

My first and primary reply is that there is a saying among programmers: "There is not now, nor has there ever been, nor will there ever be, any programming language in which it is the least bit difficult to write bad code."

This is known as Flon's Law.

The lesson of Flon's Law is that there is no point in trying to invent a programming language which can coerce programmers into writing code you approve of, because that is impossible.

The deeper message of Flon's Law is that this kind of defensive, adversarial, lock-down-all-the-doors, block-the-idiots-at-all-costs thinking doesn't lead to the invention of good programming languages. And I would say much the same about epistemology for humans.

Probability theory and decision theory shouldn't deliver clearly wrong answers. Machine-specified epistemology shouldn't mislead an AI reasoner. But if we're just dealing with verbal injunctions for humans, where there are degrees of freedom, then there is nothing we can say that a hypothetical crackpot could not somehow misuse. Trying to defend against that hypothetical crackpot will not lead us to devise a good system of thought.

But again, let's talk formal epistemology.

So far as probability theory goes, a good Bayesian ought to condition on all of the available evidence. E. T. Jaynes lists this as a major desideratum of good epistemology—that if we know A, B, and C, we ought not to decide to condition only on A and C because we don't like where B is pointing. If you're trying to estimate the accuracy of your epistemology, and you know what Bayes's Rule is, then—on naive, straightforward, traditional Bayesian epistemology—you ought to condition on both of these facts, and estimate $P(\text{accuracy}|\text{know\_Bayes})$ instead of $P(\text{accuracy})$. Doing anything other than that opens the door to a host of paradoxes.

The convergence that perfect Bayesians exhibit on factual questions doesn't involve anyone straying, even for a moment, from their individual best estimate of the truth. The idea isn't that good Bayesians try to make their beliefs more closely resemble their political rivals' so that their rivals will reciprocate, and it isn't that they toss out information about their own rationality. Aumann agreement happens *incidentally*, without any deliberate push toward consensus, through each individual's single-minded attempt to reason from their own priors to the hypotheses that best match their own observations (which happen to include observations about other perfect Bayesian reasoners' beliefs).

Modest epistemology seems to me to be taking the experiments on the outside view showing that typical holiday shoppers are better off focusing on their past track record than trying to model the future in detail, and combining that with the Dunning-Kruger effect, to argue that we ought to throw away most of the details in our self-observation. At its epistemological core, modesty says that we should abstract up to a particular *very general* self-observation, condition on it, and then not condition on anything else because that would be inside-viewing. An observation like, "I'm familiar with the cognitive science literature discussing which debiasing techniques work well in practice, I've spent time on calibration and visualization exercises to address biases like base rate neglect, and my experience suggests that they've helped," is to be generalized up to, "I use an epistemology which I think is good." I am then to ask myself what average performance I would expect from an agent, conditioning only on the fact that the agent is using an epistemology that they think is good, and not conditioning on that agent using Bayesian epistemology or debiasing techniques or experimental protocol or mathematical reasoning or anything in particular.

Only in this way can we force Republicans to agree with us... or something. (Even though, of course, anyone who wants to shoot off their own foot will actually just reject the whole modest framework, so we're not *actually* helping anyone who wants to go astray.)

Whereupon I want to shrug my hands helplessly and say, "But given that this isn't normative probability theory and I haven't seen modesty advocates appear to get any particular outperformance out of their modesty, why go there?"

I think that's my true rejection, in the following sense: If I saw a sensible formal epistemology underlying modesty and I saw people who advocated modesty going on to outperform myself and others, accomplishing great deeds through the strength of their diffidence, then, indeed, I would start paying very serious attention to modesty.

That said, let me go on beyond my true rejection and try to construct something of a *reductio*. Two *reductios*, actually.

The first *reductio* is just, as I asked the person who proposed the signal-receiver epistemology: "Okay, so why don't you believe in God like a majority of people's signal receivers tell them to do?"

"No," he replied. "Just no."

"What?" I said. "You're allowed to say 'just no'? Why can't I say 'just no' about collapse interpretations of quantum mechanics, then?"

This is a serious question for modest epistemology! It seems to me that on the signal-receiver interpretation you have to believe in God. Yes, different people believe in different Gods, and you could claim that there's a majority disbelief in every particular God. But then you could as easily disbelieve in quantum mechanics because (you claim) there isn't a majority of physicists that backs any particular interpretation. You could disbelieve in the whole edifice of modern physics because no exactly specified version of that physics is agreed on by a majority of physicists, or for that matter, by a majority of people on Earth. If the signal-receiver argument doesn't imply that we ought to average our beliefs together with the theists and all arrive at an 80% probability that God exists, or whatever the planetary average is, then I have no idea how the epistemological mechanics are supposed to work. If you're allowed to say "just no" to God, then there's clearly some level—object level, meta level, meta-meta level—where you are licensed to take your own reasoning at face value, despite a majority of other receivers getting a different signal.

But if we say "just no" to anything, even God, then we're no longer modest. We are faced with the nightmare scenario of having *granted ourselves discretion* about when to disagree with other people, a discretionary process where we *take our own reasoning at face value.* (Even if a majority of others disagree about this being a good time to take our own beliefs at face value, telling us that reasoning about the incredibly deep questions of religion is surely the worst of all times to trust ourselves and our pride.) And then what do you say to the Republican?

And if you give people the license to decide that they ought to defer, e.g., only to a majority of members of the National Academy of Sciences, who mostly don't believe in God; then surely the analogous license is for theists to defer to the true experts on the subject, their favorite priesthood.

The second *reductio* is to ask yourself whether a superintelligent AI system ought to soberly condition on the fact that, in the world so far, many agents (humans in psychiatric wards) have believed themselves to be much more intelligent than a human, and they have all been wrong.

Sure, the superintelligence thinks that it remembers a uniquely detailed history of having been built by software engineers and raised on training data. But if you ask any other random agent that thinks it's a superintelligence, that agent will just tell you that it remembers a unique history of being chosen by God. Each other agent that believes itself to be a superintelligence will forcefully reject any analogy to the other humans in psychiatric hospitals, so clearly "I forcefully reject an analogy with agents who wrongly believe themselves to be superintelligences" is not sufficient justification to conclude that one really is a superintelligence. Perhaps the superintelligence will plead that its internal experiences, despite the extremely abstract and high-level point of similarity, are really extremely dissimilar in the details from those of the patient in the psychiatric hospital. But of course, if you ask them, the psychiatric patient could just say the same thing, right?

I mean, the psychiatric patient *wouldn't* say that, the same way that a crackpot wouldn't *actually* give a long explanation of why they're allowed to use the inside view. But they *could*, and according to modesty, That's Terrible.

iii.

To generalize, suppose we take the following rule seriously as epistemology, terming it Rule M for Modesty:

> **Rule M**: Let X be a very high-level generalization of a belief subsuming specific beliefs X_1, X_2, X_3.... For example, X could be "I have an above-average epistemology," X_1 could be "I have faith in the Bible, and that's the best epistemology," X_2 could be "I have faith in the words of Mohammed, and that's the best epistemology," and X_3 could be "I believe in Bayes's Rule, because of the Dutch Book argument." Suppose that all people who believe in any X_i, taken as an entire class X, have an average level F of fallibility. Suppose also that most people who believe some X_i also believe that their X_i is not similar to the rest of X, and that they are not like most other people who believe some X, and that they are less fallible than the average in X. Then when you are assessing your own expected level of fallibility you should condition only on being in X, and compute your expected fallibility as F. You should not attempt to condition on being in

X_3 or ask yourself about the average fallibility you expect from people in X_3.

Then the first machine superintelligence should conclude that it is in fact a patient in a psychiatric hospital. And you should believe, with a probability of around 33%, that you are currently asleep.

Many people, while dreaming, are not aware that they are dreaming. Many people, while dreaming, may believe at some point that they have woken up, while still being asleep. *Clearly* there can be no license from "I think I'm awake" to the conclusion that you actually are awake, since a dreaming person could just dream the same thing.

Let Y be the state of not thinking that you are dreaming. Then Y_1 is the state of a dreaming person who thinks this, and Y_2 is the state of actually being awake. It boots nothing, on Rule M, to say that Y_2 is introspectively distinguishable from Y_1 or that the inner experiences of people in Y_2 are actually quite different from those of people in Y_1. Since people in Y_1 usually falsely believe that they're in Y_2, you ought to just condition on being in Y, not condition on being in Y_2. Therefore you should assign a 67% probability to currently being awake, since 67% of observer-moments who believe they're awake are actually awake.

Which is why—in the distant past, when I was arguing against the modesty position for the first time—I said: "Those who dream do not know they dream, but when you are awake, you know you are awake." The modest haven't formalized their epistemology very much, so it would take me some years past this point to write down the Rule M that I thought was at the heart of the modesty argument, and say that "But you know you're awake" was meant to be a *reductio* of Rule M in particular, and why. Reasoning under uncertainty and in a biased and error-prone way, still we can say that the probability we're awake isn't just a function of how many awake versus sleeping people there are in the world; and the rules of reasoning that let us update on Bayesian evidence that we're awake can serve *that* purpose equally well whether or not dreamers can profit from using the same rules. If a rock wouldn't be able to use Bayesian inference to learn that it is a rock, still I can use Bayesian inference to learn that I'm not.

7. Status Regulation and Anxious Underconfidence

I've now given my critique of modesty as a set of explicit doctrines. I've tried to give the background theory, which I believe is nothing more than conventional cynical economics, that explains why so many aspects of the world are not optimized to the limits of human intelligence in the manner of financial prices. I have argued that the essence of rationality is to adapt to whatever world you find yourself in, rather than to be "humble" or "arrogant" *a priori*. I've tried to give some preliminary examples of how we *really, really* don't live in the Adequate World where constant self-questioning would be appropriate, the way it *is* appropriate when second-guessing equity prices. I've tried to systematize modest epistemology into a semiformal rule, and I've argued that the rule yields absurd consequences.

I was careful to say all this first, because there's a strict order to debate. If you're going to argue against an idea, it's bad form to start off by arguing that the idea was generated by a flawed thought process, before you've explained why you think the idea itself is wrong. Even if we're refuting geocentrism, we should first say how we know that the Sun does not orbit the Earth, and *only then* pontificate about what cognitive biases might have afflicted geocentrists. As a rule, an idea should initially be discussed as though it had descended from the heavens on a USB stick spontaneously generated by an evaporating black hole, before any word is said psychoanalyzing the people who believe it. Otherwise I'd be guilty of poisoning the well, also known as Bulverism.

But I've now said quite a few words about modest epistemology as a pure idea. I feel comfortable at this stage saying that I think modest epistemology's popularity owes something to its emotional appeal, as opposed to being strictly derived from epistemic considerations. In particular: emotions related to social status and self-doubt.

Even if I thought modesty were the correct normative epistemology, I would caution people not to confuse the correct reasoning principle with those particular emotional impulses. You'll observe that I've written one or two things above about how *not* to analyze inadequacy, and mistakes not to make. We hear far too little from its advocates about potential misuses and distortions of modest epistemology, if we're going to take modest epistemology seriously as a basic reasoning mode, technique, or principle.

And I'll now try to describe the kinds of feelings that I think modesty's appeal rests on. Because I've come to appreciate increasingly that human beings are *really genuinely* different from one another, you shouldn't be surprised if it seems to you like this is *not* how you work. I claim nonetheless that many people do work like this.

i.

Let's start with the emotion—not restricted to cases of modesty, just what I suspect to be a common human emotion—of "anxious underconfidence."

As I started my current writing session, I had just ten minutes ago returned from the following conversation with someone looking for a job in the Bay Area that would give them relevant experience for running their own startup later:

> ELIEZER: Are you a programmer?
>
> ASPIRING FOUNDER: That's what everyone asks. I've programmed at all of my previous jobs, but I wouldn't call myself a programmer.
>
> ELIEZER: I think you should try asking (person) if they know of any startups that could use non-super programmers, and look for a non-doomed startup that's still early-stage enough that you can be assigned some business jobs and get a chance to try your hand

at that without needing to manage it yourself. That might get you the startup experience you want.

ASPIRING FOUNDER: I know how to program, but I don't know if I can display that well enough. I don't have a Github account. I think I'd have to spend three months boning up on programming problems before I could do anything like the Google interview— or maybe I could do one of the bootcamps for programmers—

ELIEZER: I'm not sure if they're aimed at your current skill level. Why don't you try just one interview and see how that goes before you make any complicated further plans about how to prove your skills?

This fits into a very common pattern of advice I've found myself giving, along the lines of, "Don't assume you can't do something when it's very cheap to try testing your ability to do it," or, "Don't assume other people will evaluate you lowly when it's cheap to test that belief."

I try to be careful to distinguish the virtue of avoiding overconfidence, which I sometimes call "humility," from the phenomenon I'm calling "modest epistemology." But even so, when overconfidence is such a terrible scourge according to the cognitive bias literature, can it ever be wise to caution people against *under*confidence?

Yes. First of all, overcompensation after being warned about a cognitive bias is also a recognized problem in the literature; and the literature on that talks about how bad people often are at determining whether they're undercorrecting or overcorrecting.[52] Second, my own experience has been

---

[52] From Bodenhausen, Macrae, and Hugenberg (2003):

> [I]f correctional mechanisms are to result in a less biased judgment, the perceiver must have a generally accurate lay theory about the direction and extent of the bias. Otherwise, corrections could go in the wrong direction, they could go insufficiently in the right direction, or they could go too far in the right direction, leading to overcorrection. Indeed, many examples of overcorrection have been documented (see Wegener & Perry, 1997, for a review), indicating that even when a bias is detected and capacity and

that while, yes, commenters on the Internet are often overconfident, it's very different when I'm talking to people in person. My more recent experience seems more like 90% telling people to be less underconfident, to reach higher, to be more ambitious, to test themselves, and maybe 10% cautioning people against overconfidence. And yes, this ratio applies to men as well as women and nonbinary people, and to people considered high-status as well as people considered low-status.

Several people have now told me that the most important thing I have ever said to them is: "If you *never* fail, you're only trying things that are too easy and playing far below your level." Or, phrased as a standard Umeshism: "If you can't remember any time in the last six months when you failed, you aren't trying to do difficult enough things." I first said it to someone who had set themselves on a career track to becoming a nurse instead of a physicist, even though they liked physics, because they were *sure* they could succeed at becoming a nurse.

I call this "anxious underconfidence," and it seems to me to share a common thread with social anxiety. We might define "social anxiety" as "experiencing fear far in excess of what a third party would say are the reasonably predictable exterior consequences, with respect to other people possibly thinking poorly of you, or wanting things from you that you can't provide them." If someone is terrified of being present at a large social event because someone there might *talk* to them and they might be confused and stutter out an answer—when, realistically, this at worst makes a transient poor impression that is soon forgotten because you are not at the center of the other person's life—then this is an *excess* fear of that event.

Similarly, many people's emotional makeup is such that they experience what I would consider an excess fear—a fear disproportionate to the non-emotional consequences—of *trying something and failing*. A fear so strong that you become a nurse instead of a physicist because that is something you

---

motivation are present, controlled processes are not necessarily effective in accurately counteracting automatic biases.

are *certain* you can do. Anything you might *not* be able to do is crossed off the list instantly. In fact, it was probably never generated as a policy option in the first place. Even when the correct course is obviously to just try the job interview and see what happens, the test will be put off indefinitely if failure feels possible.

If you've never wasted an effort, you're filtering on far too high a required probability of success. Trying to avoid wasting effort—yes, that's a good idea. Feeling bad when you realize you've wasted effort—yes, I do that too. But some people slice off the entire realm of uncertain projects because the prospect of having wasted effort, of having been publicly wrong, seems so horrible that projects in this class are not to be considered.

This is one of the emotions that I think might be at work in recommendations to take an outside view on your chances of success in some endeavor. If you only try the things that are allowed for your "reference class," you're supposed to be safe—in a certain social sense. You may fail, but you can justify the attempt to others by noting that many others have succeeded on similar tasks. On the other hand, if you try something more ambitious, *you could fail and have everyone think you were stupid to try.*

The mark of this vulnerability, and the proof that it is indeed a fallacy, would be not *testing* the predictions that the modest point of view makes about your inevitable failures—even when they would be cheap to test, and even when failure doesn't lead to anything that a non-phobic third party would rate as terrible.

ii.

The other emotions I have in mind are perhaps easiest to understand in the context of efficient markets.

In humanity's environment of evolutionary adaptedness, an offer of fifty carrots for a roasted antelope leg reflects a judgment about roles, relationships, and status. This idea of "price" is easier to grasp than the economist's notion;

and given that somebody *doesn't* have the economist's very specific notion in mind when you speak of "efficient markets," they can end up making what I would consider an extremely understandable mistake.

You tried to explain to them that even if they thought AAPL stock was underpriced, they ought to question themselves. You claimed that they *couldn't* manage to be systematically right on the occasions where the market price swung drastically. Not unless they had access to insider information on single stocks—which is to say, they just couldn't do it.

But "I can't do that. *And you can't either!*" is a suspicious statement in everyday life. Suppose I try to juggle two balls and succeed, and then I try to juggle three balls and drop them. I could conclude that I'm bad at juggling and that other people could do better than me, which comes with a loss of status. Alternatively, I could heave a sad sigh as I come to realize that juggling more than two balls is just not possible. Whereupon my social standing in comparison to others is preserved. I even get to give instruction to others about this hard-won life lesson, and smile with sage superiority at any young fools who are still trying to figure out how to juggle three balls at a time.

I grew up with this fallacy, in the form of my Orthodox Jewish parents smiling at me and explaining how when they were young, they had asked a lot of religious questions too; but then they grew out of it, coming to recognize that some things were just beyond our ken.

At the time, I was flabbergasted at my parents' arrogance in assuming that because they couldn't solve a problem as teenagers, nobody else could possibly solve it going forward. Today, I understand this viewpoint not as arrogance, but as a simple flinch away from a painful thought and toward a pleasurable one. You can admit that you failed where success was possible, or you can smile with gently forgiving superiority at the youthful enthusiasm of those who are still naive enough to attempt to do better.

Of course, some things *are* impossible. But if one's flinch response to failure is to perform a mental search for reasons one couldn't have succeeded, it can be tempting to slide into false despair.

In the book *Superforecasting*, Philip Tetlock describes the number one characteristic of top forecasters, who show the ability to persistently outperform professional analysts and even small prediction markets: *they believe that outperformance in forecasting is possible, and work to improve their performance.*[53]

I would expect this to come as a shock to people who grew up steeped in academic studies of overconfidence and took away the lesson that epistemic excellence is mostly about accepting your own limitations.[54] But I read that chapter of *Superforecasting* and laughed, because I was pretty sure from my own experience that I could guess what had happed to Tetlock: he had run into large numbers of naive respondents who smiled condescendingly at the naive enthusiasm of those who thought that anyone can get good at predicting future events.[55]

Now, imagine you're somebody who didn't read *Superforecasting*, but did at least grow up with parents telling you that if they're not smart enough to be a lawyer, then neither are you. (As happened to a certain childhood friend of mine who is now a lawyer.)

And then you run across somebody who tries to tell you, not just that *they* can't outguess the stock market, but that *you're* not allowed to become good at it either. They claim that nobody is allowed to master the task at which they failed. Your uncle tripled his savings when he bet it all on GOOG, and this person tries to wave it off as luck. Isn't that like somebody condescendingly explaining why juggling three balls is impossible, after you've seen with your own eyes that your uncle can juggle four?

---

[53] From *Superforecasting*: "The strongest predictor of rising into the ranks of superforecasters is perpetual beta, the degree to which one is committed to belief updating and self-improvement. It is roughly three times as powerful a predictor as its closest rival, intelligence."

[54] E.g., Alpert and Raiffa, "A Progress Report on the Training of Probability Assessors" (https://faculty.washington.edu/jmiyamot/p466/pprs/alpertm prog report on training o prob assessors.pdf).

[55] Or rather, get better at predicting future events than intelligence agencies, company executives, and the wisdom of crowds.

This isn't a naive question. Somebody who has seen the condescension of despair in action is right to treat this kind of claim as suspicious. It *ought* to take a massive economics literature examining the idea in theory and in practice, and responding to various apparent counterexamples, before we accept that a new kind of near-impossibility has been established in a case where the laws of physics seem to leave the possibility open.

Perhaps what you said to the efficiency skeptic was something like:

> If it's obvious that AAPL stock should be worth more because iPhones are so great, then a hedge fund manager should be able to see this logic too. This means that this information will already be baked into the market price. If what you're saying is true, the market already knows it—and what the market knows beyond that, neither you nor I can guess.

But what they *heard* you saying was:

> O thou, who burns with tears for those who burn
> In Hell, whose fires will find thee in thy turn
> Hope not the Lord thy God to mercy teach
> For who art thou to teach, or He to learn?[56]

This again is an obvious fallacy for them to suspect you of committing. They're suggesting that something might be wrong with Y's judgment of X, and you're telling them to shut up because Y knows far better than them. Even though you can't point to any flaws in the skeptic's suggestion, can't say anything about the kinds of reasons Y has in mind for believing X, and can't point them to the information sources Y might be drawing from. And it just so happens that Y is big and powerful and impressive.

If we could look back at the ages before liquid financial markets existed, and record all of the human conversations that went on at the time, then practically every instance in history of anything that sounded like what you

---

[56]From Edward FitzGerald's *Rubaiyat of Omar Khayyám*.

said about efficient markets—that some mysterious powerful being is always unquestionably right, though the reason be impossible to understand—would have been a mistake or a lie. So it's hard to blame the skeptic for being suspicious, if they don't yet understand how market efficiency works.

What you said to the skeptic about AAPL stock is justified for extremely liquid markets on short-term time horizons, but—at least I would claim—very rarely justified anywhere else. The claim is, "If you think you know the price of AAPL better than the stock market, then no matter how good the evidence you think you've found is, your reasoning just has some hidden mistake, or is neglecting some unspecified key consideration." And no matter how valiantly they argue, no matter how carefully they construct their reasoning, we just smile and say, "Sorry, kid." It is a final and absolute slapdown that is *meant* to be inescapable by any mundane means within a common person's grasp.

Indeed, this supposedly inescapable and crushing rejoinder looks surprisingly similar to a particular social phenomenon I'll call "status regulation."

iii.

Status is an extremely valuable resource, and was valuable in the ancestral environment.

Status is also a somewhat conserved quantity. Not everyone can be sole dictator.

Even if a hunter-gatherer tribe or a startup contains more average status per person than a medieval society full of downtrodden peasants, there's still a sense in which status is a limited resource and letting someone walk off with lots of status is like letting them walk off with your bag of carrots. So it shouldn't be surprising if *acting like you have more status than I assign to you* triggers a negative emotion, a slapdown response.

If slapdowns exist to limit access to an important scarce resource, we should expect them to be cheater-resistant in the face of intense competition for that resource.[57] If just anyone could find some easy sentences to say that let them get higher status than God, then your system for allocating status would be too easy to game. Escaping slapdowns should be hard, generally requiring more than mere abstract argumentation.

Except that *people are different*. So not everyone feels the same way about this, any more than we all feel the same way about sex.

As I've increasingly noticed of late, and contrary to beliefs earlier in my career about the psychological unity of humankind, not all human beings have all the human emotions. The logic of sexual reproduction makes it unlikely that anyone will have a new complex piece of mental machinery that nobody else has... but *absences* of complex machinery aren't just possible; they're amazingly common.

And we tend to underestimate how different other people are from ourselves. Once upon a time, there used to be a great and acrimonious debate in philosophy about whether people had "mental imagery" (whether or not people actually see a little picture of an elephant when they think about an elephant). It later turned out that some people see a little picture of an elephant, some people don't, and both sides thought that the way they personally worked was so fundamental to cognition that they couldn't imagine that other people worked differently. So both sides of the philosophical debate thought the other side was just full of crazy philosophers who were willfully denying the obvious. The typical mind fallacy is the bias whereby we assume most other people are much more like us than they actually are.

If you're fully asexual, then you haven't felt the emotion others call "sexual desire"... but you can feel friendship, the warmth of cuddling, and in most cases you can experience orgasm. If you're not around people who

---

[57]The existence of specialized cognitive modules for detecting cheating can be seen, e.g., in the Wason selection task. Test subjects perform poorly when asked to perform a version of this task introduced in socially neutral terms (e.g., rules governing numbers and colors), but perform well when given an isomorphic version of the task that is framed in terms of social rules and methods for spotting violators of those rules. See Cosmides and Tooby, "Cognitive Adaptations for Social Exchange" (http://www.cep.ucsb.edu/papers/Cogadapt.pdf).

talk explicitly about the possibility of asexuality, you might not even realize you're asexual and that there is a distinct "sexual attraction" emotion you are missing, just like some people with congenital anosmia never realize that they don't have a sense of smell.

Many people seem to be the equivalent of asexual with respect to the emotion of status regulation—myself among them. If you're blind to status regulation (or even status itself) then you might still see that people with status get respect, and hunger for that respect. You might see someone with a nice car and envy the car. You might see a horrible person with a big house and think that their behavior ought not to be rewarded with a big house, and feel bitter about the smaller house you earned by being good. I can feel all of those things, but people's overall place in the pecking order isn't a fast, perceptual, pre-deliberative *thing* for me in its own right.

For many people, I gather that the social order is a reified emotional *thing* separate from respect, separate from the goods that status can obtain, separate from any deliberative reasoning about who ought to have those goods, and separate from any belief about who consented to be part of an implicit community agreement. There's just a felt sense that some people are lower in various status hierarchies, while others are higher; and overreaching by trying to claim significantly more status than you currently have is an offense against the reified social order, which has an immediate emotional impact, separate from any beliefs about the further consequences that a social order causes. One may *also* have explicit beliefs about possible benefits or harms that could be caused by disruptions to the status hierarchy, but the status regulation feeling is more basic than that and doesn't depend on high-level theories or cost-benefit calculations.

Consider, in this context, the efficiency skeptic's perspective:

SKEPTIC: I have to say, I'm baffled at your insistence that hedge fund managers are the summit of worldly wisdom. Many hedge fund managers—possibly most—are nothing but charlatans who convince pension managers to invest money that ought to have gone into index funds.

CECIE: Markets are a mechanism that allow and incentivize a single smart participant to spot a bit of free energy and eat it, in a way that aggregates to produce a global equilibrium with no free energy. We don't need to suppose that most hedge fund managers are wise; we only need to suppose that a tiny handful of market actors are smart enough in each case to have already seen what you saw.

SKEPTIC: I'm not sure I understand. It sounds like what you're saying, though, is that your faith is not in mere humans, but in some mysterious higher force, the "Market."

You consider this Market incredibly impressive and powerful. You consider it folly for anyone to think that they can know better than the Market. And you just happen to have on hand a fully general method for slapping down anyone who dares challenge the Market, without needing to actually defend this or that particular belief of the Market.

CECIE: A market's efficiency doesn't derive from its social status. True efficiency is very rare in human experience. There's a very good reason that we had to coin a term for the concept of "efficient markets," and not "efficient medicine" or "efficient physics": because in those ecologies, not just anyone can come along and consume a morsel of free energy.

If you personally know better than the doctors in a hospital, you can't walk in off the street tomorrow and make millions of dollars saving more patients' lives. If you personally know better than an academic field, you can't walk in off the street tomorrow and make millions of dollars filling the arXiv with more accurate papers.

SKEPTIC: I don't know. The parallels between efficiency and human status relations seem awfully strong, and this "Market moves in mysterious ways" rejoinder seems like an awfully convenient trick.

Indeed, I would be surprised if there *weren't* at least some believers in "efficient markets" who assigned them extremely high status and were tempted to exaggerate their efficiency, perhaps feeling a sense of indignation at those who dared to do better. Perhaps there are people who feel an urge to slap down anyone who starts questioning the efficiency of Boomville's residential housing market.

So be it; Deepak Chopra can't falsify quantum mechanics by being enthusiastic about a distorted version of it. The efficiency skeptic should jettison their skepticism, and should take care to avoid the fallacy fallacy—the fallacy of taking for granted that some conclusion is false just because a fallacious argument for that conclusion exists.[58]

I once summarized my epistemology like so: "Try to make sure you'd arrive at different beliefs in different worlds." You don't want to think in such a way that you wouldn't believe in a conclusion in a world where it were true, just because a fallacious argument could support it. Emotionally appealing mistakes are not invincible cognitive traps that nobody can ever escape from. Sometimes they're not even that hard to escape.

The remedy, as usual, is technical understanding. If you know in detail when a phenomenon switches on and off, and when the "inescapable" slapdown is escapable, you probably won't map it onto God.

---

[58] Give me any other major and widely discussed belief from any other field of science, and I shall paint a picture of how it resembles some other fallacy—maybe even find somebody who actually misinterpreted it that way. It doesn't mean much. There's just such a vast array of mistakes human minds can make that if you rejected every argument that looks like it could maybe be guilty of some fallacy, you'd be left with nothing at all.

It often just doesn't mean very much when we find that a line of argument can be made to look "suspiciously like" some fallacious argument. Or rather: being suspicious is one thing, and being so suspicious that relevant evidence cannot realistically overcome a suspicion is another.

iv.

I actually can't recall seeing anyone make the mistake of treating efficient markets like high-status authorities in a social pecking order.[59] The more general phenomenon seems quite common, though: heavily weighting relative status in determining odds of success; responding to overly ambitious plans as though they were not merely imprudent but impudent; and privileging the hypothesis that authoritative individuals and institutions have mysterious unspecified good reasons for their actions, even when these reasons stubbornly resist elicitation and the actions are sufficiently explained by misaligned incentives.

From what I can tell, status regulation is a second factor accounting for modesty's appeal, distinct from anxious underconfidence. The impulse is to construct "cheater-resistant" slapdowns that can (for example) prevent dilettantes who are low on the relevant status hierarchy from proposing new SAD treatments. Because if dilettantes can exploit an inefficiency in a respected scientific field, then this makes it easier to "steal" status and upset the current order.

In the past, I didn't understand that an important part of status regulation, as most people experience it, is that one needs to already possess a certain amount of status before it's seen as acceptable to reach up for a given higher level of status. What could be wrong (I previously thought) with trying to bestow unusually large benefits upon your tribe? I could understand why it would be bad to claim that you had already accomplished more than you had—to claim more respect than was due the good you'd already done. But what could be wrong with trying to do more good for the tribe, in the future, than you already had in the present?

It took me a long time to understand that *trying to do interesting things in the future* is a status violation because your current status right now determines

---

[59] It's a mistake that somebody could make, though, and people promoting ideas that are susceptible to fallacious misinterpretation do have an obligation to post warning signs. Sometimes it feels like I've spent my whole life doing nothing else.

what kinds of images you are allowed to associate with yourself, and if your status is low, then many people will intuitively perceive an unpleasant violation of the social order should you associate with yourself an image of possible future success above some level. Only people who already have something like an aura of *pre*-importance are allowed to try to do important things. Publicly setting out to do valuable and important things *eventually* is above the status you already have *now*, and will generate an immediate system-1 slapdown reaction.

I recognize now that this is a common lens through which people see the world, though I still don't know how it feels to *feel* that.

Regardless, when I see a supposed piece of epistemology that looks to me an *awful* lot like my model of status regulation, but which doesn't seem to cohere with the patterns of correct reasoning described by theorists like E. T. Jaynes, I get suspicious. When people cite the "outside view" to argue that one should stick to projects whose ambition and impressiveness befit one's "reference class," and announce that any effort to significantly outperform the "reference class" is epistemically suspect "overconfidence," and insist that moving to take into account local extenuating factors, causal accounts, and justifications constitutes an illicit appeal to the "inside view" and we should rely on more obvious, visible, *publicly demonstrable* signs of *overall auspiciousness or inauspiciousness...* you know, I'm not sure this is strictly inspired by the experimental work done on people estimating their Christmas shopping completion times.

I become suspicious as well when this model is deployed in practice by people who talk in the same tone of voice that I've come to associate with status regulation, and when an awful lot of what they say sounds to me like an elaborate rationalization of, "Who are *you* to act like some kind of big shot?"

I observe that many of the same people worry a lot about "What do you say to the Republican?" or the possibility that crackpots might try to *cheat*—like they're trying above all to guard some valuable social resource from the possibility of theft. I observe that the notion of somebody being able to steal that resource *and get away with it* seems to inspire a special degree of horror, rather than just being one more case of somebody making a mistaken probability estimate.

I observe that *attempts to do much better than is the norm* elicit many heated accusations of overconfidence. I observe that *failures to even try to live up to your track record or to do as well as a typical member of some suggested reference class* mysteriously fail to elicit many heated accusations of *under*confidence. Underconfidence and overconfidence are symmetrical mistakes *epistemically*, and yet somehow I never see generalizations of the outside view even-handedly applied to correct both biases.

And so I'm skeptical that this reflects normative probability theory, pure epistemic rules such as aliens would also invent and use. Sort of like how an asexual decision theorist might be skeptical of an argument saying that the pure structure of decision theory implies that arbitrary decision agents with arbitrary biologies ought to value sex.

This kind of modesty often looks like the condescension of despair, or bears the "God works in mysterious ways" property of attributing vague good reasons to authorities on vague grounds. It's the kind of reasoning that makes sense in the context of an efficient market, but it doesn't seem to be coming from a model of the structure or incentives of relevant communities, such as the research community studying mood disorders.

No-free-energy equilibria do generalize beyond asset prices; markets are not the only ecologies full of motivated agents. But sometimes those agents aren't sufficiently motivated and incentivized to do certain things, or the agents aren't all individually free to do them. In this case, I think that many people are doing the equivalent of humbly accepting that they can't possibly know whether a single house in Boomville is overpriced. In fact, I think this form of status-oriented modesty is extremely common, and is having hugely detrimental effects on the epistemic standards and the basic emotional health of the people who fall into it.

v.

Modesty can take the form of an explicit epistemological norm, or it can manifest in more quiet and implicit ways, as small flinches away from painful thoughts and towards more comfortable ones. It's the latter that I think is causing most of the problem. I've spent a significant amount of time critiquing the explicit norms, because I think these serve an important role as canaries piling up in the coalmine, and because they are bad epistemology in their own right. But my chief hope is to illuminate that smaller and more quiet problem.

I think that anxious underconfidence and status regulation are the main forces motivating modesty, while concerns about overconfidence, disagreement, and theoreticism serve a secondary role in justifying and propagating these patterns of thought. Nor are anxious underconfidence and status regulation entirely separate problems; bucking the status quo is particularly painful when public failure is a possibility, and shooting low can be particularly attractive when it protects against accusations of hubris.

Consider the outside view as a heuristic for minimizing the risk of social transgression and failure. Relying on an outside view instead of an inside view will generally mean making fewer knowledge claims, and the knowledge claims will generally rest on surface impressions (which are easier to share), rather than on privileged insights and background knowledge (which imply more status).

Or consider the social utility of playing the fox's part. The fox can say that they rely only on humble data sets, disclaiming the hedgehog's lofty theories, and disclaiming any special knowledge or special powers of discernment implied thereby. And by sticking to relatively local claims, or only endorsing global theories once they command authorities' universal assent, the fox can avoid endorsing the kinds of generalizations that might encroach on someone else's turf or otherwise disrupt a status hierarchy.

Finally, consider appeals to agreement. As a matter of probability theory, perfect rationality plus mutual understanding often entails perfect agreement.

161

Yet it doesn't follow from this that the way for human beings to become more rational is to try their best to minimize disagreement. An all-knowing agent will assign probabilities approaching 0 and 1 to all or most of its beliefs, but this doesn't imply that the best way to become more knowledgeable is to manually adjust one's beliefs to be as extreme as possible.

The behavior of ideal Bayesian reasoners is important evidence about how to become more rational. What this usually involves, however, is understanding how Bayesian reasoning works internally and trying to implement a causally similar procedure, not looking at the end product and trying to pantomime particular surface-level indicators or side-effects of good Bayesian inference. And a psychological drive toward automatic deference or self-skepticism isn't the *mechanism* by which Bayesians end up agreeing to agree.

Bayes-optimal reasoners don't Aumann-agree because they're following some exotic meta-level heuristic. I don't know of any general-purpose rule like that for quickly and cheaply leapfrogging to consensus, except ones that do so by sacrificing some amount of expected belief accuracy. To the best of my knowledge, the outlandish and ingenious trick that really lets flawed reasoners inch nearer to Aumann's ideal is just the old-fashioned one where you go out and think about yourself and about the world, and do what you can to correct for this or that bias in a case-by-case fashion.

Whether applied selectively or consistently, the temptation of modesty is to "fake" Aumann agreement—to rush the process, rather than waiting until you and others can *actually* rationally converge upon the same views. The temptation is to call an early halt to risky lines of inquiry, to not claim to know too much, and to not claim to aspire to too much; all while wielding a fully general argument against anyone who doesn't do the same.

And now that I've given my warning about these risks and wrong turns, I hope to return to other matters.

My friend John thought that there were hidden good reasons behind Japan's decision not to print money. Was this because he thought that the Bank of Japan was big and powerful, and therefore higher status than a non-professional-economist like me?

I literally had a bad taste in my mouth as I wrote that paragraph.[60] This kind of psychologizing is not what people epistemically virtuous enough to bet on their beliefs should spend most of their time saying to one another. They should just be winning hundreds of dollars off of me by betting on whether some AI benchmark will be met by a certain time, as my friend later proceeded to do. And then later he and I both lost money to other friends, betting against Trump's election victory. The journey goes on.

I'm not scheming to taint all humility forever with the mere suspicion of secretly fallacious reasoning. That would convict me of the fallacy fallacy. Yes, subconscious influences and emotional temptations are a problem, but you can often beat those if your explicit verbal reasoning is good.

I've critiqued the fruits of modesty, and noted my concerns about the tree on which they grow. I've said why, though my understanding of the mental motions behind modesty is very imperfect and incomplete, I do not expect these motions to yield good and true fruits. But cognitive fallacies are not invincible traps; and if I spent most of my time thinking about meta-rationality and cognitive bias, I'd be taking my eye off the ball.[61]

---

[60] Well, my breakfast might also have had something to do with it, but I *noticed* the bad taste while writing those sentences.

[61] There's more I can say about how I think modest epistemology and status dynamics work in practice, based on past conversations; but it would require me to digress into talking about my work and fiction-writing. For a supplemental chapter taking a more concrete look at these concepts, see https://equilibriabook.com/hero-licensing.

Conclusion:
Against Shooting Yourself in the Foot

Somehow, someone is going to horribly misuse all the advice that is contained within this book.

Nothing I know how to say will prevent this, and all I can do is advise you not to shoot your own foot off; have some common sense; pay *more* attention to observation than to theory in cases where you're lucky enough to have both and they happen to conflict; put yourself and your skills on trial in every accessible instance where you're likely to get an answer within the next minute or the next week; and update hard on single pieces of evidence if you don't already have twenty others.

I expect this book to be of much more use to the underconfident than the overconfident, and considered cunning plots to route printed copies of this book to only the former class of people. I'm not sure reading this book will *actually* harm the overconfident, since I don't know of a single case where any previously overconfident person was *actually* rescued by modest epistemology and thereafter became a more effective member of society. If anything, it might give them a principled epistemology that actually makes sense by which to judge those contexts in which they are, in fact, unlikely to outperform. Insofar as I have an emotional personality type myself, it's more disposed to iconoclasm than conformity, and inadequacy analysis is what I use to direct that impulse in productive directions.

But for those certain folk who cannot be saved, the terminology in this book will become only their next set of excuses; and this, too, is predictable.

If you were never disposed to conformity in the first place, and you read this anyway... then I won't tell you not to think highly of yourself before you've already accomplished significant things. Advice like that wouldn't have *actually* been of much use to myself at age 15, nor would the universe have been a better place if Eliezer-1995 had made the mistake of listening to it. But you might talk to people who have tried to reform the US medical system from within, and hear what things went wrong and why.[62] You might remember the Free Energy Fallacy, and that it's much easier to save yourself than your country. You might remember that an aspect of society can fall well short of a liquid market price, and still be far above an amateur's reach.

I don't have good, repeatable exercises for training your skill in this field, and that's one reason I worry about the results. But I can tell you this much: *bet on everything.* Bet on everything where you can or will find out the answer. Even if you're only testing yourself against one other person, it's a way of calibrating yourself to avoid both overconfidence and underconfidence, which will serve you in good stead emotionally when you try to do inadequacy reasoning. Or so I hope.

Beyond this, other skills that feed into inadequacy analysis include "see if the explanation feels stretched," "figure out the further consequences," "consider alternative hypotheses for the same observation," "don't hold up a mirror to life and cut off the parts of life that don't fit," and a general acquaintance with microeconomics and behavioral economics.

The policy of saying only what will do no harm is a policy of total silence for anyone who's even slightly imaginative about foreseeable consequences. I hope this book does more good than harm; that is the most I can hope for it.

For yourself, dear reader, try not to be part of the harm. And if you end up doing something that hurts you: *stop doing it.*

Beyond that, though: if you're trying to do something *unusually well* (a common enough goal for ambitious scientists, entrepreneurs, and effective altruists), then this will often mean that you need to seek out the most neglected problems. You'll have to make use of information that isn't widely known or accepted, and pass into relatively uncharted waters. And modesty is

---

[62] As an example, see Zvi Mowshowitz's "The Thing and the Symbolic Representation of The Thing" (https://thezvi.wordpress.com/2015/06/30/the-thing-and-the-symbolic-representation-of-the-thing/), on MetaMed, a failed medical consulting firm that tried to produce unusually high-quality personalized medical reports.

especially detrimental for that kind of work, because it discourages acting on private information, making less-than-certain bets, and breaking new ground. I worry that my arguments in this book could cause an overcorrection; but I have other, competing worries.

The world isn't mysteriously doomed to its current level of inadequacy. Incentive structures have parts, and can be reengineered in some cases, worked around in others.

Similarly, human bias is not inherently mysterious. You can come to understand your own strengths and weaknesses through careful observation, and scholarship, and the generation and testing of many hypotheses. You can avoid overconfidence *and* underconfidence in an even-handed way, and recognize when a system is inadequate at doing X for cost Y without being exploitable in X, or when it is exploitable-to-someone but not exploitable-to-you.

Modesty and immodesty are bad heuristics because even where they're correcting for a real problem, you're liable to overcorrect.

Better, I think, to not worry quite so much about how lowly or impressive you are. Better to meditate on the details of what you can do, what there is to be done, and how one might do it.

About the author. Eliezer Yudkowsky is a decision theorist and computer scientist at the Machine Intelligence Research Institute in Berkeley, California who is known for his work in technological forecasting. His publications include the *Cambridge Handbook of Artificial Intelligence* chapter "The Ethics of Artificial Intelligence," co-authored with Nick Bostrom. Yudkowsky's writings have helped spark a number of ongoing academic and public debates about the long-term impact of AI, and he has written a number of popular introductions to topics in cognitive science and formal epistemology, such as *Rationality: From AI to Zombies* and *Harry Potter and the Methods of Rationality*.

Made in the USA
Middletown, DE
02 September 2019